Agenda for Survival

The Environmental Crisis – 2

Based on a lecture series organized
by the Yale School of Forestry with
funds from The Ford Foundation

AGENDA

FOR

SURVIVAL

THE ENVIRONMENTAL CRISIS – 2

edited by Harold W. Helfrich, Jr.

New Haven and London, Yale University Press, 1970

Designed by Sally Sullivan
set in IBM Selectric Press Roman type,
and printed in the United States of America by
The Carl Purington Rollins Printing-Office
of the Yale University Press.

Distributed in Great Britain, Europe, and Africa by
Yale University Press, Ltd., London; in Canada by
McGill-Queen's University Press, Montreal; in Mexico
by Centro Interamericano de Libros Académicos,
Mexico City; in Australasia by Australia and New
Zealand Book Co., Pty., Ltd., Artarmon, New South
Wales; in India by UBS Publishers' Distributors Pvt.,
Ltd., Delhi; in Japan by John Weatherhill, Inc.,
Tokyo.

Contents

Foreword

The Yale School of Forestry was founded in 1900 by Gifford Pinchot. Shortly thereafter he said, "The rightful use and purpose of our natural resources is to make people strong and well, able and wise, well taught, well fed, well clothed, well housed, full of knowledge and initiative with equal opportunity for all, and special privileges for none."

It is evident that over the years the primary concern of the school has been the preparation of graduate students to lead in the improvement of the quality of life by improving the standards of natural-resource management. The preservation of the environment, the balanced use of natural resources, and the informed application of knowledge for the maintenance of harmony between man and nature have been its principal aims.

In recent times the general concern about the natural environment has been voiced in the United States and around the world. The education of all the peoples on such a vast global subject as the survival of humanity constitutes a transcending duty for everyone who can make his voice heard.

The Yale School of Forestry, mindful of its long tradition and of the urgency of the crisis, is an eager participant in the continuing search for solutions. It offers an ideal forum for the exchange of ideas from many disciplines.

Not everyone has as yet become convinced that there is an imminent danger of a worldwide environmental catastrophe. The warnings of disastrous overpopulation and of vanishing natural resources are shrugged off with epithets such as "doomsday prophets."

Many—among them the oppressed, the impoverished, and the antiwar groups—are intent upon holding the public's attention until their demands are met. They frequently complain that the environmental issues are faddish and perhaps even constitute a "copout" for the complacent, apathetic majority.

Most of these views are held by individuals whose motives are just as well-meaning and altruistic as the environmentalists'. Certainly we heed the cries for genuine equality and for freedom from oppression, for permanent escape from the ghetto and a decent way of life, for enduring peace throughout the world. It is beyond reason for anyone of good will to oppose or to deny such rights and demands.

But how will these achievements benefit us or our descendants if, during their attainment, we seal man's fate by allowing his limited supply of air and water to become irretrievably poisoned, by fouling and carelessly consuming his vital but finite natural resources, by encouraging him to multiply until his planet becomes so burdened that famine and pestilence overwhelm it and all of its organisms?

We have not yet reached the point of no return, but the dire predictions are not far beyond the realm of probability if a sincere effort to secure our environment is delayed too long. We know that our deteriorating atmosphere is beginning to threaten our breathing (and surely much more). We look at our dying lakes, and we see that even the mighty oceans are in danger of becoming huge cesspools in which marine life cannot long endure. We recognize starvation, which is already claiming millions of lives in places where swiftly expanding populations are crowded into hovels or spend their lifetime on the streets, and we watch crime breeding wildly among these same pitiful masses who sometimes turn to narcotics for respite from the horrors of their environment.

The aspirations of the poor, and of those who yearn for peace, are inextricably linked to the pleas of the environmentalists because each is mutually dependent upon the others. Human society is as much of an ecological phenomenon as the life of a forest or the sea.

This volume of papers—and a similar book which preceded it *(The Environmental Crisis: Man's Struggle to Live with Himself)*—is derived from the two-year Yale School of Forestry symposium on "Issues in the Environmental Crises." It is intended to serve as a reflective examination of our ecological problems. It contains the thoughts on the environmental issues of leading authorities from such diverse fields as the applied sciences, sociology, industry, conservation, urban design, architecture, law, politics, and public or personal opinions. These suggestions may help to guide us toward solutions.

Of course, the participants in the symposium presented a wide variety of opinions expressing their personal views rather than the collective judgment of the Yale Forestry School faculty.

The symposium was instituted in 1968 by two farsighted and concerned members of the faculty of the Yale School of Forestry, F. Herbert Bormann, Oastler Professor of Forest Ecology, and Garth K. Voigt, Margaret K. Musser Professor of Forest Soils. It proved to be so successful in its first year that it was resumed during the 1969-70 academic year, this time under the guidance of former U.S. Secretary of the Interior Stewart Udall, who was serving as Visiting Professor (Adjunct) of Environmental Humanism at the Yale School of Forestry. He invited the speakers, served as moderator for each session, and delivered the initial and concluding lectures. To these men, and to all who contributed toward the success of the symposium, we owe immeasurable gratitude. These lectures were made possible by a grant from the Ford Foundation, whose continued support and encouragement are deeply appreciated.

François Mergen
Dean
School of Forestry
Yale University

Preface

In the preparation of this book and its predecessor *(The Environmental Crisis: Man's Struggle to Live with Himself)* I rolled up a tremendous debt to many individuals who cooperated without complaint.

This is particularly true of Mrs. Nancy W. Canetti of the Yale School of Forestry, who painstakingly transcribed the recorded lectures in the "Issues in the Environmental Crises" symposium to the typewritten word, and of my wife Anne for the long hours she spent in the early morning and late evening trying to produce clean, readable manuscripts from my virtually illegible editorial markings.

I must record my appreciation, too, for the invaluable aid (and comfort) given me by Professors Garth K. Voigt and F. Herbert Bormann and by Dean François Mergen of the Yale School of Forestry in smoothing my way and assuring me of the manuscripts' scientific accuracy; and by Mrs. Jacquelin L. Steinfield, the Dean's secretary and a pillar of support for me in several difficult moments.

Finally, mention must be made of the kind and courteous assistance accorded to me by the lecturers whose spoken words I changed into essay form and by Mrs. Anne F. Wilde, the busy Science Editor of the Yale University Press, for her matchless advice on many occasions.

Harold W. Helfrich, Jr.
New Haven, Conn.

Total Environment:
A New Political Reality

Stewart L. Udall

What is the use of a house if you haven't
got a tolerable planet to put it on?
Henry Thoreau

This discussion is designed to set the stage for the second part of
The Environmental Crisis. The reader should be warned that I am
a politician, and politicians are glib by nature; they like to ram-
ble, they will pontificate at the drop of a question, and they
usually do not like to be pinned down. This opening statement
will therefore be diffuse because our environment is a diffuse,
all-embracing subject.

In this volume a broad spectrum of topics will be discussed by
ecologists, economists, enlightened industrialists, demographers,
politicians, designers, urban-ghetto experts, and others. For the
total-environment approach of "the new conservation" demands
an overview of man and of all his manifold activities that are
determining the habitat of tomorrow in this country and on this
planet.

A decade ago "conservation" was concerned with specific resources: the preservation of forests, wildlife, parklands, or whatever. Today we recognize that man has been engaging in activities
that affect the whole life system of the planet; instead of focusing
on a specific resource, therefore, we must paint on a canvas that
might be a river valley, a region, a continent—or the planet itself.
Ecology is an overarching science. It demands that we be holistic
in our approach.

*Stewart L. Udall, a long-time advocate of natural resources conservation,
was Visiting Professor (Adjunct) in Environmental Humanism in the Yale
School of Forestry during 1969-70. He is Chairman of the Board of The
OVERVIEW Group, an international consulting firm working to create a
better environment for mankind. He served four terms as a U.S. congressman from Arizona and was Secretary of the Interior throughout the Kennedy and Johnson administrations. He is author of* The Quiet Crisis *and*
1976: Agenda for Tomorrow.

This concept that we have evolved, which we call the environment, rejects the dichotomy of city and countryside, just as it seeks to balance and harmonize the works of man and the works of nature. Man's environment, we have belatedly realized, is a totality—the result of all those technological activities and policies and decisions that determine the qualities and ambience of the "house" in which we spend our lives. The best efforts of the old conservation—as vital as they were, and are—to provide better management of a specific or a single tract of land in an untrammeled state were doomed to fail because an upwind pollutant or upstream waste or a persistent pesticide or sonic boom can destroy the very values thought to be "saved" by earlier generations.

In an era of massive intrusions by technology no part of the environment is, or can be, an island. Naturalists have been trying to drive home this lesson for a long time; but it took the machines and processes of twentieth-century technology, thrusting disruptive forces into every part of the biosphere, to prove their point unmistakably and to make ecology a central science of our time.

Consequently this volume must range over a broad front. We cannot illuminate the real issues of the environmental crises unless we encompass and attempt to interrelate all of the contemporary vectors that are shaping the habitat of tomorrow.

We are now in a dying decade. As a conservationist, I would characterize the 1960s as a distorted period in which environmental erosion and environmental awareness both increased. An examination of the principal events and trends of the 1960s suggests some of the reasons at the root of this paradox:

It was the decade that witnessed the first—and let us hope the last—nuclear confrontation of the so-called superpowers. (Mankind survived, we should soberly note, because of restraint by President Kennedy and Chairman Khrushchev and their advisers. At the brink they recognized that civilization would not survive a nuclear holocaust. History may one day point to October 28, 1962, as the most sane moment of the entire decade—an awesome experience that gave mankind a reprieve in which to learn more about the common interest in compromises that would make future existence possible.)

It was the decade that saw the largest increment in Gross National Product (GNP) in United States history. It marked the successful use of economic controls in this country to reduce sharp swings in the business cycle. It witnessed the production of more machines, goods, and services than any decade in history. But it was also the decade in which we produced more effluents, poisons, and pollutants than in any comparable period in our national life; there was more spoliation of our country in the 1960s than ever before.

It was also the decade in which American technologists and astronauts put men on the moon.

And it was the decade in which an Asian land war consumed much of the energy, blood, and treasure that we needed to solve social and environmental problems here at home.

It was the decade in which we built more miles of highway than ever before and achieved an unparalleled level of individual mobility. But it also saw the instrument of that success—the motor vehicle—create unprecedented congestion and pollution.

It was the decade in which our failure to make a multiracial society work was certified by conflagrations and social tensions in most of our large cities.

It was the decade in which, for the first time, an awareness entered the American mind that most of the large cities were sick and the overall environment was in a condition of crisis.

(It was also, in my view, the decade that was robbed of its finest leaders by the work of assassins.)

The overpowering paradox of the 1960s, then, is the sharp contrast between the high-level performance of our economic-industrial-technological system and the most serious social-environmental crisis in our history. Of course the predicament of the blacks and other minorities, the cancerous condition of cities, and the erosion of our resources were not attributable solely to the disordered priorities and uneven performance of the 1960s.

Other undisciplined generations made their contributions to blight and befoulment—but the men and women of the 1960s had to endure the results and begin to devise plans for a counter-strategy of cleanup and control.

The condition of man's environment at any given time is, therefore, a result of all the basic decisions, priorities, goals, achievements, and failures of the past. For example, increases in automobile ownership and air pollution go together, just as disordered military commitments and decaying cities are interrelated. We now painfully concede (though Washington would not admit it, at least while I was there) that the Vietnam War left no money to tackle the many current problems that cause severe social strains and confront us with environmental erosion that affects everyone's lives. We rarely discussed it, but there was a direct relationship between our achievements in outer space and the erosion of the inner space of earth, between the vast increase of GNP and the similar increase of GNW (Gross National Wastes).

If one is to judge by some decisions of the new administration in Washington, the priorities of the past continue to operate: $600 million is available to subsidize the supersonic transport (SST), but there are no funds for urban open space of "last chance" seashores and parklands; we are manufacturing an anti-ballistic missile system, but the federal government has reneged on its commitment to fund a full-scale fight against water pollution; we plan to spend $10 billion on a space platform, but money for model cities and low-cost housing is lacking; and we can allot only a few million dollars for population-control research and education programs at the same time that we are allocating $7 or $8 billion for military research and development.

Our triumph in sending the first men safely on a round trip to the moon gave us a moment of national pride. It was an important event for our "world prestige," as we call it. But I think we can look back on it now with a little less giddiness. I must confess that I had reservations about the space program even when President Kennedy made the decision for a crash effort in this area. I have always had feelings of ambivalence about the program. To be sure, I have a pride in the skill, the talent, the courage that were exhibited; but I wondered whether as a result we might end up as a people with more hubris and whether we might be more in the grip of a deadly euphoria about instant salvation by technological "miracles."

I would prefer that we could look back on the '60s as the decade in which we made a multiracial society work. But we denied ourselves this satisfaction. We went to the moon; that was our landmark achievement. But what does this say about our national purpose and our priorities?

At the time of our first lunar-landing triumph, President Nixon, in a euphoric moment, exclaimed: "Nothing has done more to change the world." As an earth-minded environmentalist, I disagree. The truth is that this feat has had, and will have, little effect on the condition of man. I suspect we are going to find that, particularly as the third and fourth loads of moon rock return, we will become bored. The lifeless lunar surface has little to teach us about life.

C. P. Snow pointed out in an August 26, 1969, *Look* magazine essay, "The Moon Landing," that despite the spirit of adventure generated by the moon mission, the solar system is a dreary and dead place—a dead end for human aspirations. He predicted that in a few decades we will be forced to turn inward, to realize that the ultimate frontier is the mind of man and the society of men on this planet.

So let us accept the cliché that our achievement in space *did* demonstrate that we have the potential to do "anything we want to do." But that does not decide issues of national priorities. It does not assist us in redefining national aims and national purpose.

When one surveys the scientific community today, it is revealing that the optimists about the future are engineers and physical scientists, such as Glenn T. Seaborg, Edward Teller, and Wernher von Braun. The pessimists are biologists and ecologists, such as René Dubos, Barry Commoner, and Durward Allen. Seaborg writes ecstatically about the potential of "extended man"[1] at the same time that Durward Allen is issuing the gloomy warning, "In the sum total of their ecological malpractice, the elders are

leading humanity toward the damnation of the lemmings."[2]
This should not relieve our anxiety as we face the complex
growth decisions that will shape our future.

In my view, preeminent among the issues in the environmental
crises are the following:

Population Control

If, as a nation, we could exhibit the wisdom and restraint
needed to effect a leveling off of population, it would offer real
hope for our tomorrows, for it would give us the resources and
time we desperately need here and abroad to begin large prob-
lem-solving projects that would enhance the future of man.

It is a paramount assumption of American life today that,
willy-nilly, our population will double and then redouble in the
next century. I believe the fight for a life-giving environment will
inevitably and irretrievably be lost if we follow this course. The
margins of life will be narrowed to the point at which only an
endurable environment will be an achievable objective.

If Henry David Thoreau were to return, how many areas in New
England would delight his eye? Martha's Vineyard, or the Alla-
gash country in northern Maine, you say? Perhaps; but surely he
would be appalled by the ravages of "progress."

We have probably altered the face and character of this country
more in this decade than our forebears did in the entire nineteenth century. And we have altered it invariably with dehumanizing effects. The struggle of the environmentalists of tomorrow,
if we are going to have a doubling and redoubling of population,
will be not for a superior environment but for a life-defeating,
second-rate environment. If this is so, the most appealing, most
humane aspects of life will be contaminated, obliterated, or
rationed. No zoos or museums or plastic flowers or clever enter-
tainment can compensate for the dehumanizing effect of huge
increases in population.

My generation has readily accepted the inevitable-growth
assumption; but unless I mistake the signs, our children do not,
and therein lies the main hope.

A creative pause in procreation—a nonproliferation treaty with ourselves—may be the best hope of the next decade. A leveling off of population would offer a historic opportunity to the American people. It would occur if new concepts of parenthood, new demands for a quality environment, a more humane approach to abortions, and a life style of restraint were to replace our present acquiescence in a program of unlimited growth.

The current national policy favors growth; our tax policies and our social attitudes encourage it. But without any leadership from their elders the younger generation has been evolving a slow-growth policy. The birth rate has turned down, despite the predictions of demographers. It has gone below the low point of the 1930s—and were it not for medical advances that have increased longevity, we would have zero population growth today. Why has this situation occurred? Because the young people want to know more about themselves and their readiness for marriage before they wed; they want to wait until they are sure they are prepared to be parents before they undertake parenthood; they want to have fewer children and assure them the gift of more care and love and attention as part of a higher life style.

"Less is more" should be our unswerving slogan if we hope to achieve a quality environment. This is more than a consummation to be wished. It is a paramount necessity if we are to have a fighting chance to solve our social problems, to rescue the cities, and to raise true living standards to a higher level.

Rescuing Urban Environments

The plight of the urban dweller was discerned by George H. Gallup recently when his organization ascertained that only thirteen out of every hundred people living in our largest cities would remain there if they had a free choice.[3] That statistic tells us much about the decline of urban livability. Our most expensive, time-consuming environmental task is the reshaping and restoration of the American city. We have failed miserably as builders of balanced, beautiful cities. It will require revitalized and reformed governments, a new kind of participatory democracy, designers who have the capacity to think and plan for whole cities and regions as total environments, and conservationists who will demand, neighborhood-by-neighborhood and block-by-block, the restoration of the amenities we have destroyed.

This will be a vast and challenging enterprise. But handsome, vibrant, joyful cities have always been the highest expression of any civilization. Sooner or later we must undertake the task—or resign ourselves to materialistic mediocrity.

To drive this point home, let me relate what I call my tale of two cities. Some months ago I went to Houston, Texas, and rode into the city with its mayor. He had just returned from Guadalajara, Mexico—one of the loveliest cities in our hemisphere. Economically Houston is a rich city; Guadalajara, by comparison, is poor.

But they have equivalent populations, and the mayor quite naturally asked questions and gathered statistics about their similarities and differences. Guadalajara, he found out, has the same number of gardeners as policemen. Guadalajara is a city of squares and plazas. It has a rich legacy of historic buildings that give it a special flavor and character. The mayor learned that it has 185 fountains of all sizes and is building another 100 in the next three years. Much of the life of the city takes place in these public places, where water and beauty and music create a serene atmosphere for a gentle, happy populace. Houston, by contrast, has very few plazas—and hardly any public fountains or gardens. Guadalajara, the mayor learned, had only seven homicides in the preceding year. Houston had something like 230.

I do not relate this story to suggest that if our cities had more gardeners, we would have fewer homicides. What I am trying to say is that wealth alone does not make any city an attractive, enjoyable place to live. A handsome city is far more than bustling business or soaring skyscrapers. People love—and live well—in cities that offer them places to work and play, that give constant pleasure as well as profit. Design that fits the human scale, not the convenience of automobile owners, is the beginning of public happiness. That is one of the lessons of this tale of two cities.

Civilizing Technology

Do we have the ingenuity and desire to make the machine enhance, and not destroy, the overall environment? Can we reorient the same technology that has fouled and slashed and despoiled much of our environment to restore, cleanse, and recreate it?

The time has come for us to demand these fruits of American technology:

1. A pollution-free, noiseless automobile.
2. Systems of sensible, efficient mass transit to replace the tyranny of the auto. (Individual mobility is one of the advantages that we prize most; it is one of the central features of American life today. But look at the price we pay for this kind of mobility: congested cities choked with foul air. We have driven urban mass-transit systems to the wall by our policy of all-out support for the auto; and the final human cost is the 53,000 who die each year and the over 3 million who are injured, wounded, scarred, or maimed for life.)
3. Processes to recycle and reuse our solid wastes instead of dumping them into all corners of the country. (We are a generation of dumpers: in the last twenty-five years we have thrown more wastes onto our land and into our waters than in all our previous history.)
4. Low-cost processes to cleanse our dwindling supplies of fresh water for reuse.
5. Noise-suppression devices to soften the voice of urban-industrial America.
6. Innovative air-pollution control devices to lower the level of air contamination.

In the years ahead we should beware of engineers bearing conventional gifts. On the other hand, we should applaud those inventors and designers who show us how to use the machine to ease our environmental ills.

Avoidance of Ecocatastrophes

We must begin to heed the warnings of the ecologists. They are the ultimate accountants, and we ignore their counsel at our peril. · "We are practicing—not by intention but irresponsibility—a kind of biological warfare against nature, ourselves, and especially our descendants," bacteriologist René Dubos has written.[4] Henceforth, if we assume a moral duty toward future generations, we must give the closest scrutiny to those activities that disrupt or tamper with the ecosystem of the planet. And the burden of proof should rest on advocates of conventional growth to demonstrate that their projects or processes do not damage the environment.

Fortunately such questioning has begun. In recent times we have seen doubts raised about the Atomic Energy Commission's nuclear explosions in the Aleutian Islands; the fight against DDT and other long-lived pesticides appears to be coming to a climax; and even the SST is in some trouble.

The Value Revolution

There are hopeful signs that a value revolution is under way in this country that might change the aims and attitudes of the American people. The depredations of public and private polluters and spoilers of the environment are arousing angry opposition; vigilante citizen groups are forming, and politicians who have never shown any interest in conservation are suddenly uncertain champions of the cause.

We must evolve a national outlook that will reject the old attitudes that made production more important than people, that has treated engineering efficiency as an end in itself, that has ignored the environmental claims of posterity.

From the beginning of the Industrial Revolution we have operated on the basic assumption that any highly industrialized society would, ipso facto, be ugly and unclean. We assumed without question that our rivers should be sewers, our air filthy, our landscapes littered. This, we thought, was the price we had to pay for the standard of living and level of production that would make us prosperous. We have at last begun to question that assumption. I believe we must discard it altogether if we hope to repel the blight that threatens to engulf us.

There are indications that more and more citizens are revolted by the imbalance of a system that creates wealth by destroying the beauty and appeal of the country. The belching smokestack is no longer the badge of industrial success. Poorly planned, large-scale projects of the kind that have long been applauded as "progress"—dam building, the filling of bays and estuaries, the construction of freeways and new airports, the erection of new power stations, and the drilling of offshore oil fields—are being opposed in all parts of the country. Questions concerning quality are being asked of those who advocate more-of-the-same expansion.

Moral indignation and alarm over the soiled and second-rate life setting we are creating for future generations have characterized the "new conservation" of the 1960s, along with a refusal to accept further degradation of man's environment as the price of a new round of affluence. The late Walter Gropius summarized the fears of environmentalists with his assertion that we were "sacrificing the tree of life for a commercial sales spiral."

Such doubts raise basic issues about our national values and national purpose. What is true wealth? How does one measure the worth of a society? What should be the ultimate aims of a rich and gifted people? If the cause we call environment is more than a fad, such questions about values will not only dominate our dialogue in the years ahead but will alter our life styles as well.

The times demand nothing less than a sustained, life-centered effort to reshape the attitudes, laws, and institutions that have produced the mess that is man-made America. If we fail to act, we will richly deserve the unclean country and ugly, uninhabitable cities that will be the end result of another generation of mindless growth.

Many eminent ecologists are profoundly pessimistic about the future. There are days when I share their forebodings, when it is hard to search the horizon and find hopeful signs. To the extent that I am an optimist, my hope derives from three new currents in American life.

The first is the quite recent convergence of the family-planning movement and the conservation cause. This overdue alliance (of Margaret Sanger and Henry David Thoreau, one might say) is encouraging in that it signals an awareness that the surest way to save nature and promote life is for men and women to contemplate a nonproliferation treaty with themselves.

The second promising note of restraint comes from the courts. The young lawyers who have established legal beachheads in their fight against environmental degradation have rendered a great service to the country. Judges who have opened the doors of courts to the arguments of outraged citizen groups have done much to encourage the idea that our institutions are flexible enough to react to the environmental crisis. It is too early to say whether the judiciary will accept the argument that the Constitution protects *life* as well as liberty and property, but there is satisfaction in the circumstance that the law—once the most standpat institution—may become an ally of restraint.

A third, and perhaps most hopeful, indication of ecological sanity is the convictions of youth. The young adults of the 1960s who have rejected the population-increase-is-good policies of my generation (and have reduced the national birthrate by nearly one-third) deserve an accolade. Their honest anger over the fouling of *their* nests, their questions about the materialistic yardsticks of conventional growth have been cause for guarded optimism.

I like to believe that once the Vietnam War is liquidated, the students' energies and anger will turn upon those who are defiling the American earth. If the new generation should demand policies—and politicians—who put a life-giving environment ahead of "progress," we might see the kind of historic turnaround that could save the land. Is this a consummation beyond contemplation in the 1970s? Let us hope not.

These papers will not answer the questions I have raised. The agenda for survival which will be adopted, or avoided, by the American people will do that. What this symposium can do, I hope, is to define the crucial issues and to point out some of the possible solutions. If we do that, the rest is up to you.

References

[1] Glenn T. Seaborg, "Uneasy World Gains Power over Destiny," *New York Times,* January 6, 1969, pp. 141, 146.

[2] Durward L. Allen, "Population Resources and the Great Complexity," Population Resources Bulletin No. 29, August 1969.

[3] George H. Gallup, Special Study for the National Wildlife Federation, July 1969.

[4] René Dubos, "Is This Progress . . . or Self-Destruction?" *New York Times,* January 6, 1969, p. 142.

Human Nonproliferation:
A Political Responsibility

Edgar Berman, M.D.

Unprecedented human population growth is no longer an abstract sociologic equation to be studied academically, nor simply a frightening specter of famine and disease, nor just the widening economic discrepancy between the rich and the poor. It is all of these and more—with a devastating cumulative effect. It can no longer be approached delicately and deviously to avoid the diminishing and last-ditch religious strictures, nor is there time to dawdle at the present inadequate pace of voluntary free choice.

The compromise of some democratic principles now may save the more basic freedoms later.

Humanity's growth in numbers is the most overwhelming and urgent social and ecological issue ever faced by the world. Today it touches every facet of every human life. It is the major factor in spreading our modern blights of poverty, pollution, and crime, and it is bordering on irreversibility. It can no longer be merely an academic project for sociologists, scientists, or economists. It *must* be accorded the highest priority for national politics and international statesmanship, for it is a matter of global proportion, threatening world order. It is an emergency situation demanding emergency measures.

The dereliction of responsibility in the first century after English political economist T. R. Malthus (1766-1834) theorized that population increase exceeds the growth in means of subsistence can be excused on the grounds of lack of relevance—at that time—and, of course, a lack of proof. During the past five

Dr. Edgar Berman of Lutherville, Md., a noted research surgeon, served as a special assistant on health problems for Vice President Hubert H. Humphrey. He was Director of the Population Program, Agency for International Development (AID), and a participant in the U.N. World Population Conference at Belgrade in 1965. He was an observer at the Third Session of the Ecumenical Council in Rome, the Health, Education and Welfare Task Force on Vietnam, and the White House Task Force on Medical Care for the Aged.

decades, however, the crudest aggregate figures in the most conservative estimates tell the story in terms that are equally understandable to laymen, scientists, and political leaders. Yet, social
scientists have shown serious professional interest for little more
than a decade, the economists for half that time. Some of the
great international economists had absolutely no interest in the
population problem's link to the economic woes of the world as
recently as three years ago. The politician, of course, has been
alerted just lately.

What spotlighted the crisis for these groups? I think it was a
combination of the post-World War II computerized statistical
population analyses, our burgeoning welfare problem, the deteriorating quality of life in the industrialized nations, and (mainly) a
revival of interest—developmental rather than exploitative—in the
less-developed nations. After about fifteen years of technical and
financial assistance to developing nations, the common conclusion among economists was that population growth controls
per capita income more than does a reasonable developmental
capacity; in turn this relationship affects social progress and political stability. Within the wealthier nations both the professional
and lay public became aware of the fact that the quality of urban
life (and urban life comprises supposedly 70 percent of the
United States population) diminishes as the quantity increases,
regardless of the society's affluence.

Population overgrowth in the already developed nations is
obviously a problem of too much, as against too little in the
developing countries. As an example, the growth in population in
America is taking its toll not only of our standards and culture
but even of our nervous systems. Our life is more complicated by
a dependence on technology in the home, in the daily nerve-
wracking bumper-to-bumper driving on our roads, and in the
holding patterns experienced above our airports. Our schools and
colleges are more crowded, with worsening education. Our sick
must wait weeks for medical treatment. We can no longer bury,
hide, or destroy our waste products. Pollution and toxification
are facts of life. Our inner cities are crumbling. The proximity of
each of us to the others has caused tensions and mental aberra-

tions that have put us at odds with ourselves and aloof from our neighbors. In the Western World our democratic institutions have grown unwieldy to the point of stagnation; our elected officials are at such remote strata that confidence in the democratic process is waning, and in this process the citizen becomes more and more at the mercy of omnipresent bureaucrats and less of an active participant in the regulation of his own affairs.

Our culture is becoming more impersonalized because it must keep expanding to encompass more people, and our lives are transforming to greater involvement with machines than with humans. We are gripped by a gargantuan fright when whole cities are rendered helpless by a sudden power failure. Man feels small and lost—and life becomes more frenzied and automatic, but less meaningful.

The pressure that produced this cold, distant, nerve-stretching, mechanized existence is PEOPLE—more and more and more people.

Some of the awful effects of the increasing population in affluent nations are so incipient and subtle that they are not felt until it is too late. But the "other two-thirds" of the world experiences no such subtlety, for there the end product of overpopulation—stark, naked misery—is out in the open; it is a nightmare too prevalent to be hidden, and it is intensifying too rapidly to be stopped. This unhappy majority of the world is personified by a pot-bellied, uneducated child, staring vacant-eyed from a filthy hovel. We have all seen it in person or in pictures many times: a mother with a child in arms, at foot, and in belly, and her family's provider earning less than $100 a year. This scene, too, bodes repetition generation after generation, for that average annual $100 income must be further shared every year that the population growth rate just equals or surpasses the productive capacity. The agony must get much worse if, as in Latin America, 200 million people will add 100 million others in the next fifteen years, another 100 million in the following ten years, and still another 100 million in the five years thereafter.

At its best, what gigantic productive machine of a nation, what flexible culture, what political system can assimilate another 300

million people in a scant thirty years—even at a quasi-humane
level? Such a situation cannot possibly be alleviated by amateurs
and specialized academicians. This common problem for developed or underdeveloped regions has now reached proportions
involving every facet of almost every country's life. It must be
approached quickly by the power that administers nations. That
is *political* power.

A recent publication featured an article entitled "Can India
Make It?" My answer is a large NO! No matter the protestations
of India's Population Minister Sripati Chandrasekhar, who was in
the United States recently and said his country is making progress
with voluntary birth-control programs. No nation or group of
nations in Latin America, Asia, or Africa can "make it" with, at
best, a haphazard token of limitations based on pure volunteer-
ism. My categorical assertion is made without taking into account
alarmists' predictions of famine and wars of survival, although
these may occur. I say that these nations cannot "make it" in the
sense that living is more than bare survival, just an animal existence. The meaning of life is more than breathing and eating at a
minimal level and reproducing at a maximum.

India's case clearly illustrates the problem of respecting democratic rights and personal freedoms of the individual at the expense of the individual himself. It points out the inadequacy of a
voluntary approach—even through a governmentally controlled,
duly publicized, duly financed, and duly organized system of
reduced fertility that will spend $100 million this year and *still
regress.* Although it has made some inroads, if India's program—
dependent on the voluntary efforts of the citizens—could double
over the next ten years (a problematic undertaking), progress
would still be slight. Social planners predict a promising effect,
but promising is not good enough at this stage of the game.

Even *small* backward nations, such as those in Central America
with populations under five million but with an annual population growth rate of 3 to 4 percent, will find it impossible to solve
their dilemma by persuasion. When the limited financial resources
of these nations are used for consumption rather than production
for 40 to 50 percent of the population (who are children for at

least fifteen years), no rise in per-capita income is possible. There can be no rise in educational standards. There can be no rise in welfare. There can be no progress so far as the individual is concerned.

Highly literate small nations with skilled productive labor, capital, and strong governmental birth-control programs may gradually overcome their population problems. This progress has occurred in Korea and Formosa, but they are specialized cases, and they have particular advantages, such as high literacy and skilled labor that other countries do not have. With large population masses such success stories as those of Formosa and Korea are absolutely impossible. Voluntary hit-and-miss programs cannot touch the overwhelming annual increments of new people which, in fewer and fewer years, double in geometric progression. A world order reveals a large flaw in its system if it allows this type of self-destruction to occur because it is rendered impotent by the relative superficiality of certain ethical, religious, or ideologic considerations—when a solution is at hand.

No one can doubt the effectiveness in the past ten years of the "promotion" of planned parenthood. It has been estimable. But, in effect, it was still just a "promotion." Although hundreds of millions of dollars have gone into such programs in the past five or six years, fewer than 10 percent of the nations have an official population policy and fewer still implement and program for it. We have a form of policy in this country; it is involved mainly with education—which is important; with research—which is important; with changing of attitudes—which is important. But of the five million underprivileged people in this nation, the program has affected less than 100,000 mothers in their productive years.

The worldwide population growth has hardly been dented by such programs. The average size of families has not been altered, and the discrepancy between the rich and the poor still widens. Outside of the totalitarian nations (which have really begun to tackle their problems), the reason for this lack of results is the timidity of the world leaders—a timidity that regards unlimited productivity to be a human right even to the point of world breakdown. Whether in rich nations or in poor nations, enormous increases of people—at a certain threshold of progression relative to their productivity—*must* be detrimental to all. Despite the sizable effort already expended, little can be foreseen to make the necessary difference in population in the next ten years. By then the problem will be out of hand.

Much of this time lag and much of this gradualism (time is now the crux of the problem) have been self-imposed because of certain moral and ethical principles supported by political and religious institutions in our free society.

Since the population dilemma has become overt and since effective means to combat it have been discovered, controversy has ensued as to its political nature and the appropriate extent of government intervention. In the past few years governments have become involved in improving the availability of education and measures to limit births on a basis of freedom of choice. Beyond this point the subject is usually still considered too sensitive, too sacrosanct, too volatile for interference, even though it limits, deprives, and even incapacitates some two-thirds of the world, and threatens the comfort and security of the rest. Ideological and religious leaders have said, "Hands off this private decision," and their warning has been the major intimidating factor in facing the problem. Nobody really *knows* that legally limiting their reproduction would be a freedom that couples would guard preciously; it might be. Actually, the ready acceptance of birth control by women educated to its advantages connotes the contrary, but few national leaders have shown enough courage to intrude on the decisions (or lack of decisions) of this sexual unit to test it. The limitation of reproduction by law, even for the good of the unit itself and of society as a whole, has never been tried. Free nations especially have taken it for granted that the number of progeny a couple has—either by plan, ignorance, or neglect—is their business and their prerogative, regardless of the effect on the rest of their fellowmen.

Yet why should this be when other unintelligent human tendencies, foibles, and fallacies have been contravened on the basis of harm to the collective whole? So much of past polemics in defense of freedom of unlimited reproduction, especially by the body politic, has been couched in the most democratic rhetoric for the most noble purposes. It is questionable whether the real reasons are not more cultural and psychological. For we, the developed and educated nations, supposedly unshackled from our sexual inhibitions and taboos, are still subconsciously in the mental milieu of our Puritan and Victorian ancestors. Our thoughts and conversation still skirt the problems of venereal disease, premarital sex, and even sex education. We still place credence in the myth of the maternal instinct—mother's place is in the home (and we discriminate in commerce to keep her there)—and we indulge in the orientation of little girls to vicarious motherhood through the medium of the doll. However, the matter of number is rarely stressed with these toddlers, and the adolescent or adult female is usually vague about her reasons for wanting children—and more vague about how many she hopes to have. Ask the average thirteen-year-old if she wants to have children. Why, of course. The question is ridiculous! How many want three boys and four girls, three girls and four boys, and why do they want seven? They do not know. Then ask an adult the same questions, and *you get the same fuzzy answers!*

In this modern world of ours we still respect the show of male sexuality, his virility through fertility. Actually the male sense of progeny is vestigial. Generally children are almost a neutral side effect of a couple's too frequent, irresponsible gamble against the inevitable or the male's acquiescence to wifely insistence.

I have been with politicians long enough to know that, no less than others, they are prone to such cultural and psychological influences. Although they (and other apologists) know that the sexual act is as primitive as nature itself, they speciously attempt to identify the production of life with intellectual decisions and individual rights. Sex and its human side effect may be idealized and romanticized, but the following three truisms abide:

1. Decisions regarding family size are not made in bed.
2. Procreation is a rarely discussed subject between men and women in most of the world.

3. Generally, without guidelines or goals, the size of a family is determined more by default through whimsy, ignorance, and/or irresponsibility and indolence than by purpose.

On the other hand, the sexual mores and taboos established by ancient philosophers, laws, and religious dogma did produce a necessary façade of order concerning the age of consent, marriage, adultery, illegitimacy, and carnal knowledge. From them the family emerged as the most stable basic unit of social organization.

I think the family is dying fast. As the past rigid mores and myths of sexual beauty, privacy, and intimacy have crumbled in our unromantic and realistic world, the product of creation by the most animal of passions comes to be regarded less nobly by our present generation. To a large degree this situation has evolved through the supersophisticated challenges to the definition of freedom in a democratic society. With the emergence of license for this new sexual freedom, the creation of life is regarded purely as a by-product of a biologic function; yet its limitation is still considered a sacred issue. For these and many other reasons (affluence, permissiveness, dependence on psychiatry, parental selfishness, and so on), the family as a stable social institution is disintegrating. Parental abdication by the most recent adult generation in itself has helped to produce a new breed, guided and motivated by their peers; it is reasonable to question whether this authority may not be a poor substitute by any measure of parental failings.

It seems that we have come full circle, from the primitive sexual freedom and comparatively short family life of the animal, through the rigid order producing social and legal taboos and codes, on through a challenge of full sexual freedom based on democratic principles, and finally back to the jungle. With this change the hard bedrock of unwritten rules and ethics of family has eroded. The progeny of a couple is held in contact with the family mostly by material—but also by functional—dependency (as with the animal); and this period of time seems to be growing shorter and shorter. Some anthropologists and sociologists say the motive for family (beyond the couple) is strong, but this assertion has been disproved by statistics in this present generation; indeed, it promises to get weaker.

Yet—even with sex free of past strictures and considered as just another physiological function, and with moral and legal restrictions such as age and marital status gone, and with the family unit fading—homage is still paid to the production of life as a sacred matter of conscience, a reflection of freedom of the individual, and one of the basic tenets of a free society!

The free choice of the individual to reproduce in an unlimited fashion has been the essence of the political argument against even voluntary population planning, much less population limitation by alternative means. Sociologists lean toward idealization of the momentous personalized decision (rarely made) that is still sanctified by the Church; its apotheosized aura is attributive mostly to ancient dogma and of doubtful relevance to life in the twentieth century.

Besides the practices influenced by culture, psychology, and democratic forces, the Church also still has an effect—more on the politician, it seems, than on its own constituency. The sociologists formerly were more prone to probe and study and be scientifically objective (but socially aloof) about population overgrowth—with no urgency and few solutions. Today they are more oriented toward action and more committed to solving the problem. The economists, too, have come to realize that development in the backward nations is helped more by a population decrease than by an equivalent capital increase, and now they are all out for the cause.

By contrast, the Catholic Church took a giant step backward for mankind in the 1968 encyclical, *Humanae Vitae,* on birth control. Aside from its essence, the encyclical was a terrible tactical mistake; it has backfired. If the decision were a difficult moral and theological one, involving church tradition and doctrine, all that was necessary was to do—nothing. The sanction of birth control has not been unpopular with the Catholic laity (more than 70 percent use some method of control), and it has strong support from high ecclesiastical and lay intellectuals. As an official United States observer to the third and fourth sessions of the Second Vatican Council, I noted that the Papal Commission was quite positive in that leniency regarding new contraceptive methods was condoned!

Now *Humanae Vitae* is with us, causing a deep schism among the rank-and-file clergy and a confusion of conscience among the laity. In developed nations a majority of Catholics still continues to practice nonsanctioned birth control. But in Catholic developing nations, for the time being, the encyclical has hurt the Church as much as it has the nations involved. It has further weakened an almost moribund church structure and reduced its influence on previously disenchanted parishioners. It will further deplete the almost bare coffers now supported by an indigent constituency in huge areas, such as Latin America. Although this papal decision was of moral and economic importance to the further retrogression of Church vitality, it also has a temporary braking effect on political leaders and clergy who were ready to change directions. In a time (and especially in a region such as Latin America) when every day counts, this is certainly "the pause that depresses." It is ironic, in a sense, that the decision emanated from Italy, home of the Holy See: Italy has one of the lowest birth rates in the world (about 0.6 to 0.7 percent). Four other Catholic nations of Western Europe have similarly low population growth rates; France, Spain, Portugal, and Belgium record a population growth rate at least one-third lower than the United States. I doubt that these low figures obtain by an act of divine providence or that abstinence (a Church-sanctioned method) is prevalent in France and Italy.

An interesting point of logic arises in reference to the limitation of intrusion by the established order. The Church precludes effective control by edict in what it calls a "sensitive and private" matter, to the detriment of the family and society. The educated middle- and upper-class Catholics in the aforementioned nations reject the edict mainly on the basis of enlightened self-interest. Then the state (at a more distant relation to the individual than the Church) is loath to intrude on this selfsame decision to limit progeny when a large proportion of a population has risked excommunication on its own initiative to practice birth control.

Political leaders are now cognizant of all these facts, although only recently acceding to popular demand for birth control on a voluntary basis. They have also seen the abysmally sluggish results of simple appeal to self-interest when this vital subject has been left to the individual will. Usually, but not necessarily, the least interested group is in the low and middle economic circumstances, responding to no appeal of long-term self-interest, much less to that of the commonweal. They should react to offers of substantial financial recompense. Despite widespread national propaganda for an economically rewarding family life and the achievement of national goals, India is still plagued by the whim of the lowest common denominator in the male-female relationship. When the sound logical, scientific, economic, and political presentations compete with lust, apathy, customs, clichés, irresponsibility, and stubborn ignorance—the arguments for birth control lose every time. Education, persuasion, and promises make a certain impact on a reasonable percentage of burdened families, but the incentives have proved to be insufficiently tangible in the long pull for most of them.

The great issue made by political leaders over avoiding what they label "an intrusion on connubial decisions" is in a certain sense an evasion born of uncertainty and timidity. It is unconscionable and unrealistic to leave this "decision" (or lack of one) to propagate without limit to the conscience of individuals of all degrees of mental and emotional competence. The act upon which hangs the ecological balance of humanity spells life itself for some; for others it means a frustrating depression of the quality of life. It is too large a price to pay for the luxury of an individual free choice that is too rarely used, even by those who can.

In the final analysis, this small liberty may destroy more essential freedoms. The world has seen the pressures of population densities propagate increasingly restrictive regimes that gradually snuff out total freedom. The mental torpor, anxiety, and depression of the crowded life provoke a frustrated disinterest in democratic franchises and distant administrative processes. The largest population masses (the Soviet Union, China, Latin America—with India as the exception) have accepted totalitarianism with a corresponding deadening of freedom. Paradoxically, Marxist-Leninist doctrine was anti-Malthusian, but now for many years the Soviet Union and China have led the world in population control—without inquiring as to the individual's decision.

Most of the world's governments support the infringement of personal freedom for such purposes as national security—to the point of sacrifice of life. They have access, dictate guidelines, and proscribe various activities in personal and corporate finance. They ration the essentials of life in times of war, and the United States has even prohibited by law the consumption of alcohol at one stage in our recent history. Governments have also imposed child education against the will of many people at one point in history and have passed legislation to require vaccination and quarantine for public protection. All of these laws, rules, and regulations are now taken for granted, but at one time they were considered an encroachment on civil liberty and were fought tooth and nail. It is an evasion of public responsibility and a political travesty to consider as less serious the control of individual actions that threaten the well-being of all mankind.

Unlimited fertility influences every aspect of the diverse problems and interrelationships of peoples in all nations. It is quite apparent that the rationale for a strictly voluntary planning approach cannot be tolerated much longer. Inexorable time and the invincible mathematics of the problem provide the proof. After a century of warning, a quarter-century of neglect, and a decade of an effort so infinitesimal and timid that it is too shameful to admit, the only choice lies in noncoercive but effective alternatives. Now the task will involve astronomical costs, vast administrative organizations, stringent laws, and generous incentives. It will probably necessitate the abrogation of certain personal prerogatives, cultural traditions, and religious doctrines. Political means and political power in this human crisis must quickly take over with hard new dimensions and new directions, and cannot allow the specious carping associated with due process in the old traditions.

Simply and bluntly, no matter how well the voluntary or government agencies feel they have progressed (and I have been on the inside of both), and despite whatever momentum they have generated, their achievements do not come fast enough. No matter what deep inroads India's program has made, it cannot catch up by the present methods. (The program is moving, but the target is going faster.) No matter what help the Church gives at the parish level and regardless of the Catholic laity's acceptance of birth control, it is too late to temporize on theological morality. And no matter the federal government's doubling of funds each year both at home and abroad; its program has not and will not work fast enough subject just to voluntary acceptance. There is no time for further experimentation; the problem is too far gone to "wait and see." There must be directional changes now or never. All people must be advised as to limits of reproductivity, their marriageable age, and the availability of means to prevent or intercept unwanted children. People must be educated and motivated, and the whole process of limitation of births must be made easy with substantial incentives.

The big question is not whether these steps *should* be taken, but whether they *can* be taken. Is it politically feasible to act at this time, and do we have the administrative and technologic means to accomplish the task? These questions should be answered first by the developed nations in which the best possible chance lies for a quick success.

In the United States candidates for public office in 1940 mentioned population only when pressed to the wall—and sometimes not then. In the 1950s and early '60s a few senators, such as Pennsylvania's Joseph S. Clark and Ernest Gruening of Alaska, went all out in calling for controls. Former Secretary of the Interior Stewart L. Udall and his brother, Congressman Morris Udall of Arizona, stuck their necks out on the same subject when it was difficult to do so. Now, at the beginning of the 1970s, advocation of birth control is no longer considered a political liability; strangely enough, today it is generally only the Catholic legislator who softpedals the issue. Realistically one must respect a politician's principal duty to himself, which is to be elected. It must be

understood that when election campaigns are involved, controversial issues are dangerous. The subject of birth control no longer
falls into that category; now it is discussed openly by most public
officials, whether in Congress or in other national forums. They
have been educated to the problem and to its needs, and they are
deeply concerned. However, they have also felt the inadequacy of
the present haphazard voluntary system, although that is not to
say that they would support a stronger one. In view of the
progress in the past six years, some professional circles believe the
limitation of families to two children would be received even with
less hostility than population planning was six years ago. The
then president—a Catholic—formally noticed the problem favor-
ably only in 1963. Since then, two other presidents have made
strong statements, and Congress has raised appropriations—from
$400,000 in 1964 (buried at the time in a euphemistic guise that
only politicians could dream up) to possibly an open appro-
priation of almost $200 million in 1970—with no public dissent.

More than 70 percent of women in the reproductive years of all
faiths (over 60 percent of Catholic women) use contraceptives in
the United States today. A poll taken in 1964 showed that more
than 87 percent of all men and women supported government
responsibility in this "most private of human functions." United
States programs in birth-control education and motivation are
generally targeted to the minority poor. In spite of this approach,
the majority middle and upper levels (untargeted) have taken to
birth control on personal motivation alone. The change in abortion laws at the state level is a psychological step forward, as is
airing of the controversial issue of sex education in the schools.

All these changes have generated enough evidence to show that
public policy pertaining to a more forceful limitation of progeny
might possibly be ready for change. It is also uncertain that political leaders' constituents would consider federal intervention inimical to their democratic prerogatives, especially as urban growth
gets to problem proportions. Of course the political feasibility
would be enhanced by a great program of public education in
sexual knowledge and the issues of population with the aim of
changing attitudes toward family size. The term "control" in the

United States today is quietly bruited about, just as population planning was ten years ago. The Church in America has become much less vehement in its resistance to population limits, and the younger, educated clergy (receptive to some form of birth-control program) might well favor a definite limitation of family size. In a Catholic nation like Colombia, for instance—where Church and state are almost one—the Church has quietly gone along with a national policy and program using United States funds that now encompasses something over 75,000 women of child-bearing age. This attitude has given encouragement to other political leaders, including those in the United States.

I believe that an effective population program throughout the world is feasible, especially if it is started in such a great nation as the United States, which is geared to good management. I think it could be accomplished rather easily. Lack of skilled administration has been one of the principal weaknesses in underdeveloped countries, especially in India.

Real population limits would undoubtedly be productive economically. The basis of a rise in human pride and welfare is relative to population decrease. It is really zeroed in on per capita income, which increases education, which increases capital formation, which increases the standard of living. Economically, population limitation would show a high return. It has been estimated that a $150 million investment in the United States would cut in half our annual $4.5 million welfare budget within ten years. In underdeveloped nations, it is claimed, a dollar used for population control would be equivalent to $100 in developmental investment. In these underdeveloped nations 65 percent of total investment is usually devoted to maintaining the per capita income (25 percent in developed nations). For instance, $5 billion in India and $2 billion in Brazil are the resources annually absorbed by population growth alone!

From the technical aspect, most experts believe that the present methodology (the pills and the intrauterine devices—and these are becoming more and more effective) presents no problems for a feasible worldwide control program.

Then we come to the moral, ethical, and philosophical issues.

Would this brand of program be accepted? I think it would be much more acceptable to the American people, as evidenced by the ready acceptance of planned parenthood—a tremendous step forward that took forty years. There will surely be debate and controversy over its coercive nature, but the average modern American has been educated to the necessity of federal and state controls in such areas as consumer protection and the need for regulatory agencies. He has felt the power and abuse by large corporations and realizes that only the federal government is large enough to control them. In the past few decades not only has he felt this; he has had an increasing contact with the government through Social Security, Medicare, welfare, employment, poverty, and other agencies. From this it could be conjectured that he would be much less afraid of government intervention and more amenable to limitation of his family.

Americans know that poverty among such affluence in this land is amoral. They are surely troubled by the ethical aspects of over a million illegal abortions a year (in some Latin American nations there are more illegal abortions than live births). Professor Garrett Hardin of the University of California (Santa Barbara) claims that of the three million or more children born per year in our country, more than one million are unwanted.

What of the philosophy of limitation as it relates to the person and the state? There are too many examples in American lives of restriction of individual rights for the public good, which the citizens accept. Americans have seen that the results of human reproduction are no longer the concern of only the two people involved, nor of their families, nor of their nation, because the rate of reproduction in one section of the world has repercussions concerning health and welfare for every family in every hamlet on the globe. This highly touted "most private decision" must first be presented to reveal the full public reaction. It may be more or less resisted than one would think now, but mass education may help in the attainment of a positive viewpoint.

The effectiveness of legal population limits can only be shown when it is tried, and it can validly be expected to be many times more effective than the present system.

Even if a plan of population control is feasible in wealthier nations, with a strong possibility that it could also be effective in the developing nations, the laws and measures needed to attain the quickest results must be considered. This is not difficult because many of these measures have been suggested before, and some are now utilized in a few nations. They exclude contraceptive technology, academic research, and the extreme, far-out, almost science-fiction measures.

One of the most important plans to limit populations prior to coercive controls is incentives—to governments, to their subsidiary divisions, and on down to individuals. At the lowest level there are less appealing negative plans of taxation and punishment as well as more attractive positive programs with financial and other benefits.

Cash farm subsidies in the United States have shown that financial incentive is a powerful force in changing age-old habits. Even in a country as primitive as Afghanistan, which has virtually no communications system, a double reversal of wheat growing to cotton and back to wheat was accomplished within a period of three years. The illiterate farmers had a single incentive: a financial subsidy. Incentives in factory production and tax credits for corporations have similarly helped to control national economic trends. The communist nations showed some years ago the necessity for incentive in their lagging farm-industrial cooperatives.

Of the laws and measures to be considered, I stress these few:

1. The quickest way to limit fertility is to delay marriage. (This sanction is now in force in Red China.) At present in our country minimum age laws for marriage exist in every state, generally around the age of sixteen. I think it should be raised by federal law to eighteen for the female and twenty-one for the males.
2. Incentives for even later marriages by prepaid insurance policies for a number of years, bonuses, wedding subsidies, and savings certificates could be subsidized by a small general tax that would easily be repaid in just a few years.
3. Abortion would be allowed to prevent illegitimate births of

unwanted children before and after marriage. (If the child
were wanted, all incentive payments would be abolished.)

4. There could be annual cash stipends equivalent to at least
one-half of what a child costs the various levels of government—that is federal, state, and municipal; and couples
would be paid at those levels for every year of a childless
marriage during the child-bearing period. This is the most
important part of the incentive plan. An average child costs
the governments about $6,000 a year in the U.S.A.

Tax and welfare benefits might include scholarships for the first
two children; reversal of benefits to favor unmarried persons and
childless couples, and those with only two children; and pensions
with educational benefits for poor people who have two or fewer
children.

Promotion of females with equal opportunity into the labor
force by incentive to industry is important. The male has kept the
female shackled to the crib too long; it is time for her to get
away. The educational factor alone is significant, as evidenced by
the percentage of women who go to schools of higher education,
not to mention commerce. Certainly commerce is conducted on a
discriminative basis so far as the female is concerned.

Along with all those types of incentives, the educational program must be intensified for both the adult and the underadult.
The public must thoroughly understand the world population
problem and how it affects every United States citizen; it must
learn the plans and stages of a global program.

Obviously population limitation must encompass almost every
nation to have effective political results. National and international political considerations are of prime concern to this aim.
Concomitantly a worldwide campaign would help individual
political leaders to sell their program in their own nations. The
effect of such a global crusade could be denied by few individuals
or countries. It would also refute malicious arguments concerning
the suppression of ethnic groups, nationalities, or ideologic
cliques. Placed in the framework of the United Nations as the
second major goal (next to peace, as it has been described by

Secretary General U Thant), the issue would attain a supernational plane, which might help to avert extended and bitter national debate for internal political gain.

The initial stages are likely to be the most difficult. Quicker success could be expected for many reasons if the United States were to initiate the incentive program first. Movement would be essential on many fronts simultaneously. If the premise of population limits could be agreed upon (and that aim alone would probably occasion a major debate) by those leaders of the present successful congressional movement in population planning, a bipartisan majority might be available. Laws must be passed and executive orders given, and the most urgent action is the swift establishment of a population agency with all the national prestige and international negotiating powers of the Disarmament Agency—for it is of equivalent importance.

All national and international programs must come under this agency. A national and international educational program of unprecedented scope must be aggressively pushed. Voluntary agencies must be included in the crusade, and the program must be pressed simultaneously by an equivalent agency (already being considered with funds of $100 million) in the United Nations. The United States agency, however, must also concentrate on immediate bilateral agreements to build a consortium, not only to bolster its own raison d'être, but also to give the worldwide commitment in the United Nations a head start.

Such a consortium of founder nations—most of whom have been the leaders in the voluntary movement—should not be difficult to convince. They are such nations as Japan, Germany, Great Britain, and India, even France, Korea, Formosa, Sweden, and Denmark. The Soviets, who now have a quasi-control program, markedly reducing their growth rate, should by all accounts go along with the idea, since it could only accrue to their financial gain and promote stability in their sphere of influence. The population-control program has no military and little international political significance. If the Soviets do cooperate (and I see no reason why they should not), the problem will be minimal in the United Nations. With the satellite nations easily following the lead of the Soviet Union, developing nations would be greatly influenced to join.

The developing nations—the largest problem area—will need not only moral support, but also incentive (the developed countries could budget their own incentive control). Although the national appeal for their own social and economic well-being is gradually being accepted through the planned-parenthood program, in this type of voluntary program what the people gain is too far away (if ever attainable) and the political risk (especially in Latin America) is about the same as with a population-control program. The administrative, technological, and financial investment is greater for the broader control program, but the return is much quicker.

Financial incentives to nations even by a bilateral agreement have never been tried, and certainly not by a multilateral organization such as the United Nations. This latter factor may prove to be just the political ingredient necessary to induce nations to try it. Many nations may react better to a faster control program, in which the people may live to see the results, than they did to more gradual planning. In this speedier system the World Bank and other international funds (which have recently established population limitation as an integral part of the developmental armamentarium) must play a much more important role. This control program involves vast sums of money, but with better and quicker results than the voluntary plan and an assurance of repayment.

About four years ago I participated in an International Co-operation Year symposium, where I suggested extending "bilateral and multilateral investment loans and grants for development over and beyond the average to those nations who adopt a population planning program [which practically no nation had then] and thus not only assure a successful investment but a bettering of the human condition. This gambit, I must say, will require more than international cooperation; it will require international courage, forthrightness, and leadership."

Today there may have to be many different plans of a similar nature for different national population programs, but the essence of the incentive would be larger developmental loans that are commensurate with the control program undertaken; that is, the larger the program undertaken, the larger the loans for developmental process. Interest rates would be reduced proportionately to each decrement leading to the stabilization of population; for example, with a 10 percent population decrease annually, the interest rates on loans would go down by an equivalent amount—and that is considerable. Multilateral, technical, and administrative assistance would be instituted, and special loan funds would bolster individual incentive at a basic level.

The success of the program would ultimately rely on a generous individual incentive, which must be closely equivalent to at least one-half of the per-capita income for each proved sterile year; the rest of the program—with modifications—must be the same as that which I have described for developed nations. (Generally, with education, help, food, clothing, and the like, the cost of each child to a government is at least one and a half times the per-capita income.) Administratively each local and state unit showing a population decrease would also get incentive developmental loans and grants on conditions similar to those at the national level. This entire package would create capital, employment, and better living conditions; it could pay for itself in less than a decade. It would put nations less fortunate than we on the road to development and self-subsistence. History has shown that each rise in per-capita income makes incentive programs less and less necessary; economic stability and growth produce automatic population limitations.

These proposals are just a broad outline of the possible means of achieving a stable, or zero, population growth rate within a time limit before irreversibility. Even with a strong population policy, as opposed to the gradual-planning program, time is of the essence. It is self-deception to think that the present voluntary system will work fast enough. Prevention of famine and wars of survival are not the issue here; the issue is the quality of human life, as opposed to the degradation of animal subsistence.

Present means of population control have failed to prove speedy or large enough for the general good, although they reflect

the democratic freedom of choice. Laws and measures of doubtful infringement on civil liberty could possibly save our world,
but they are resisted because they *may* be inimical to that personal freedom. As a problem involving every facet of society and
as a gambit that will deeply involve not only laws but administration by government and dealings with other governments, the
solution is a matter that must be the ultimate responsibility of
politicians and statesmen.

Some form of more aggressive population limitation will eventually be necessary, if not absolutely mandatory—worldwide. The
stringency of the measures and the effect on the "human right"
of productivity will vary in direct proportion to the time lag in
control operation. There must be continued faith in the willingness of man to limit his individual will for the good of the majority.

DDT and the Environment

Charles F. Wurster

It is not sufficient to worry about the environment without clearly defining its difficulties. I am going to attempt here to define the pesticide problem—particularly as it concerns DDT. Many people have taken a position against DDT, but it is important that they know *why*. Perhaps such knowledge will put us in a better position to do something constructive about the problem. Actually, the DDT question has implications considerably beyond itself. In terms of environmental problems, it is rather unusual and may serve as a model system in some ways. It is a particularly serious pollution problem—indeed, one of the worst we have.

We know a great deal about DDT, although the price of learning has been very high in terms of environmental damage. Hopefully, we are not going to have to learn so much about every single environmental problem before we take intelligent action to solve it. It has taken scientists twenty-five years to put together the story of DDT.

It is my hope that the DDT issue can serve as a spearhead or mechanism for finding new ways to solve environmental problems, that it will open a door or a hole in the wall through which other problems might pass—problems about which we are presumably even more ignorant than we are about DDT.

In discussing DDT, the first approach should be from a theoretical standpoint. I wish to consider the physical and chemical properties of the molecule in a fairly simple fashion to explain some of the behavior of DDT in the environment. If a few simple properties of DDT had been considered twenty-five years ago, we

Charles F. Wurster is Chairman of the Scientists Advisory Committee, Environmental Defense Fund (EDF), and Assistant Professor of Biology at the State University of New York at Stony Brook. His research interests center on the physiological and ecological effects of pesticides on birds, the interrelationship of avian lipid and pesticide metabolism, and lipid biochemistry—especially phospholipids. He is a leader in the EDF campaign to create, through litigation, a body of legal interpretations for natural-resource conservation and abatement of ecologically perilous situations.

37

might not have fallen into quite such an environmental mess. After its properties are considered, it will probably become clear that much of the insecticide's resultant environmental behavior is understandable and may even be predictable in some cases. The effects of DDT's widespread usage are not quite so astonishing as they might at first appear. After those general statements, I will examine several situations, emphasizing breadth of subject matter rather than depth, to demonstrate the properties of DDT in operation.

DDT is a relatively stable material, but it does break down under certain conditions. Microorganisms can break it down; so can liver tissues and various insects' and undoubtedly other tissues, as well as certain environmental conditions. One of the routes of breakdown is from DDT to DDD, which only differs from DDT by a hydrogen instead of a chlorine atom. DDD is generally less stable than the DDT from which it came; it therefore decomposes more rapidly than DDT and goes on through several intermediates to DDA, an acetic acid derivative with a higher water solubility than DDT that can be excreted in the urine. This, then, is the main pathway for the degradation and elimination of this biologically active material.

Another pathway of environmental significance is that from DDT to DDE. Resulting from a simple dehydrochlorination to give a double-bonded compound, DDE is more stable than the DDT from which it came; it seems to back up in the environment and accumulates. Analyses of fish, bird, and human tissues show that DDE almost always constitutes anywhere from 60 to 95 percent of the DDT residues—"DDT residues" being jargon for the three compounds together: DDT, DDD, and DDE. DDE is probably more widespread than any other synthetic chemical on earth; it turns up almost everywhere.

The environmental behavior of DDT can be explained by the presence of four properties, all combined in one molecule. Modification of any one property would produce a very different situation in terms of environmental behavior.

1. DDT is a biologically active material in two different ways:

a. It is broadly active within the animal kingdom, being either toxic or active in one way or another to a great diversity of animals, ranging from the target insect to all the insects, the rest of the arthropods, and all five classes of vertebrates: fish, amphibians, reptiles, birds, and mammals. There is even some activity within the realm of plants.

b. Its activity is broad not only in terms of animal species, but also in terms of mechanisms. DDT is a nerve poison; it unstabilizes nerves. A high enough dosage produces tremors and death. This mechanism is how it kills insects, birds, and other organisms. In the last ten years other mechanisms in addition to nerve toxicity have been found. We now know that DDT is an active estrogen. (This fact may or may not be of much environmental significance; my own opinion is that it is not.) It also is an enzyme inducer. It induces liver enzymes—a fact that would appear to be of considerable environmental significance. It inhibits certain other enzymes—and this fact, too, may have environmental importance. DDT is also carcinogenic—capable of producing cancer; the significance of that finding is obvious. We have a molecule, then, that is enormously active biologically. If we contaminate living systems with it, we may not know *what* is going to happen, but we can very well predict that *something* is likely to happen.

2. DDT residues are very stable or persistent materials. They do break down, but not fast enough to keep us out of environmental trouble. Once we have used DDT, its residues remain in the environment, and we tend to be stuck with them for a long time. Nobody really knows their exact half-life in the world environment, but it is clearly many years.

3. The mobility of DDT residues is quite significant. One might hope that an insecticide will stay on the target area, but DDT departs. Although it has a finite vapor pressure and water solubility, both are extremely low. Initially these traits gave people the impression that DDT would stay

where it was put because it would not wash away. They overlooked, however, the earth's enormous volume of air and water, which can carry quite a bit of DDT at exceedingly low concentrations over a period of time. Other properties substantially enhance the ability of air and water to carry the material. Since suspensions are formed in both air and water, DDT does not have to be in solution to move. It also adsorbs to particulate matter, especially soil particles, which can erode and wash downstream in the watershed, eventually reaching the oceans. Similarly, particulates are picked up by the winds and carried about the world in the atmosphere. Finally, the material has the interesting property of co-distillation with water. This fact means that when water evaporates and DDT is in the vicinity, the DDT goes with the water. If we placed a beaker of water on a bench and suspended in it ten parts per billion of DDT, by this time tomorrow there would be only about five parts per billion; the other half would have escaped into the air as the water evaporated.

We therefore have a number of ways by which DDT residues can be transported by air and water currents to all parts of the earth. It comes down in the rainfall, and it occurs in the air wherever anybody has looked, even in remote areas. Contaminated Antarctic animals afford an example of the material's capability for distant journeys. The air over Barbados, after filtration and analysis, disclosed the presence of DDT, DDE, and dieldrin, even though this air had traversed several thousand miles of ocean.[1] Similar cases have been recorded in a number of other circumstances and locations. It is therefore hardly surprising that DDT is distributed all over the world.

4. The solubility characteristics of DDT are environmentally important. We cannot minimize the importance of the fact that DDT is a material with an extremely low water solubility—one of the lowest known for any organic chemical—while it has a very high solubility in lipids (fatlike organic materials). As a consequence, DDT is not going to remain in

the inorganic environment but will be transferred into the organic. Because all living organisms contain lipids in which DDT is more soluble, they accumulate it. Therefore, it will not get lost in the oceans or remain in the soil and air but, instead, will be funneled constantly into food chains. Organisms thus become contaminated from an environment that may often appear to be uncontaminated but actually contains a very low amount of DDT.

Obviously we have a molecule with a rather unusual combination of properties, posing a unique problem. Any time we find these properties in a compound, we can anticipate that it will behave similarly to DDT in the environment and will produce similar effects. If DDT were not so broadly active, contamination would be innocuous to nontarget organisms. If it were not so stable, it would break down before it got very far away from the site of application; with the passage of time it would break down and not reach and contaminate the sea as it has. Parathion, for example, has the other properties of DDT, but it is unstable and thus, even though an extremely toxic insecticide, it will never contaminate an ocean. If DDT were not so mobile, it would stay where we put it. Finally, if DDT had different solubility characteristics, it would not be constantly accumulated by living organisms.

With these general theoretical considerations in mind, let's now go out into the environment and examine a number of cases to see how DDT and its residues actually work in the real world.

During the last thirty years or so the eastern United States has been plagued by Dutch elm disease, a fungus transmitted from one elm tree to others by bark beetles. An attempt to control it with DDT by controlling the bark beetles has been largely unsuccessful. Dutch elm disease can be very effectively controlled by sanitation; but DDT, nevertheless, has been used on a very large scale in the last ten to twenty years.

When we spray DDT up into the elm trees, the mist blower produces very fine droplets. Part of that DDT mist, of course, escapes into the air and flies away to other parts of the world. The rest of it comes down and contaminates the soil. The various organisms living in the soil accumulate the DDT. When ground-feeding birds eat these soil organisms, large numbers become poisoned fatally.

Meanwhile flying insects also become contaminated; whether from larval forms that hatch into adults or from the elm trees directly, they also carry DDT residues and cause a substantial die-off of birds that feed in the treetops. In some cases such a die-off in a community can approach 100 percent. Of course the rate depends on the number of elms and on how much DDT is applied.

In 1965 I moved from Dartmouth College to the State University of New York at Stony Brook, where I was closely acquainted with George Woodwell of nearby Brookhaven National Laboratory. Woodwell was also interested in DDT, and together we studied a salt marsh on Long Island's south shore. We knew that the Suffolk County Mosquito Control Commission had been using DDT on the marsh for at least ten years. Presumably a lot of DDT was available to various organisms in residence on the marsh.

We ran something in excess of 200 analyses in the summer of 1966 on soils, grasses, and many kinds of organisms. The marsh averaged about a pound of DDT per acre. In the whole group of analyses there was but a single zero—only one analysis in which we could detect no trace of DDT. It was a sample of mud from forty centimeters under the surface of the marsh.

Another environmental characteristic of DDT that is important to appreciate and that follows directly from its properties is the phenomenon of biological concentration, often called biological magnification. It means that DDT's concentration becomes greater as it moves *up* a food chain. An easy way to visualize this phenomenon is to imagine a large fish eating many small fish. The large fish excretes the metabolic remains of the small fish but retains much of the DDT. As it eats more and more of the smaller fish, the DDT accumulates within the large fish. When large and small fish from the field are analyzed, therefore, one finds that the large fish contain a much higher concentration of DDT than the smaller fish on which they prey. This effect occurs at all trophic levels in the food chain; the higher you go, the greater the amount of DDT. Not only is it being absorbed into food chains, but it is also being carried up those chains toward the carnivores at the top. We should expect, therefore, to find the highest concentrations of DDT in carnivorous organisms, especially large fish and birds.

At the end of the summer of 1966 Woodwell and I found that, by arranging our marsh analyses in the order of increasing DDT concentration, we had essentially put the food web together.[2] Biological concentration occurs under most circumstances—on land, in a coastal situation such as the marsh we investigated, or in the ocean.

We estimated that in our own marsh the water contained fifty parts per trillion of DDT. Two steps up the food chain the zooplankton contained a hundred times more DDT than the water, while shrimp feeding on zooplankton were four times higher in DDT content than were the zooplankton. Smaller fish, such as minnows and silversides carried about one-fourth to one part per million (ppm) of DDT—concentrations five to ten times higher than the zooplankton on which they were presumably feeding. The larger fish, among them the pickerel and needlefish, have one or two ppm of DDT—again five or ten times higher than the small fish. Birds such as terns contain from three to ten ppm of DDT, about ten times higher than the small fish on which they feed. Finally, at the top of this particular food web, we see the large diving ducks, such as mergansers and cormorants, which contain from twenty to thirty ppm of DDT, about ten times higher than the larger fish they eat.

Thus, within a food web these residues move from bottom to top. From water, soil, or air to the carnivores at the top of food chains, the concentration of DDT frequently is concentrated by one to ten million times.

These biological concentrating mechanisms are apparently not yet understood by some government agencies that spend large quantities of money conducting monitoring programs on water and soil. Those are the wrong places to look. Water and soil analyses produce tiny concentrations that allow a feeling of complacency, with the conclusion that DDT is not accumulating in the environment. We cannot monitor water quality by analyzing water; we must analyze organisms, preferably those well up the food chain.

A few years ago I did some studies at the Woods Hole Oceanographic Institution in which the photosynthesis of marine phytoplankton was measured where DDT had been added to the water in the parts-per-billion range.[3] The data indicated that as DDT was added to the water, the rate of photosynthesis was decreased. (Photosynthesis is the process whereby green plants absorb carbon dioxide and the energy from sunlight, producing organic nutrients and oxygen. All animal life on earth is dependent on this process.) By the time we reach eight or ten parts per billion of DDT in the water, the photosynthetic rate is diminished to about three-quarters of normal; as the DDT concentration goes higher, the photosynthetic rate goes lower. Since these experiments were done, others who have worked in the field have confirmed the findings in both marine and freshwater systems.

What are the environmental implications of these results? (I find it difficult to extrapolate from an Erlenmeyer flask to an ocean.) There is no evidence that DDT is reducing the rate of photosynthesis in the ocean, nor that DDT is present there in comparable concentrations. In local areas, I think it means that if DDT reaches these concentration ranges, it will inhibit the whole base of the food chain. I believe it also indicates a likelihood of manipulating the species composition of the phytoplankton community because it is selectively toxic. Since it does not exert the same toxic stress on all species, it could aggravate problems of eutrophication (overenrichment that leads to algal blooms). It could increase algal-bloom problems where certain species that are not good food organisms could become predominant. If this should occur, the species composition of the whole food chain might be changed.

From what I have said about the properties of DDT, one would predict on purely theoretical grounds that it would eventually be transferred from its application sites on the land to the ocean basins by way of watersheds and by fallout from the air. In the oceans it should not remain in the water itself, but would be absorbed into food chains and would work its way toward the top. To find it, then, one would look for DDT in large fish or carnivorous birds that feed at the tops of oceanic food chains.

A few years ago there were indications that DDT was turning up in some tuna and a few other large fish, but data were scanty. About that time I had a letter from ornithologist David Wingate in Bermuda, who reported that the Bermuda petrel was suffering reproduction problems. He did not understand what was the trouble with this rare oceanic species, but he suspected that pesticides were somehow involved. In view of the properties of DDT and its residues and the similarity of the petrel's symptoms with those of some terrestrial birds, I suspected that DDT residues had contaminated the food chain of the petrel.

It is of interest to examine the ecology of the Bermuda petrel because it shows how remote it is from that cornfield in Nebraska where DDT may have been applied. The petrel is a bird that spends its whole life at sea. So far as anyone knows, it never comes within sight of any continent except to breed on some islets off the main island of Bermuda. During breeding season it comes and goes only by night. It stays in a burrow ten or twenty feet long, with its nest chamber at the end of the tunnel. Even if the islets had been treated with DDT, the pesticide would not contact the bird. These islets never have been treated, however, with DDT or any other insecticide. When the bird is not in its nest chamber, it is feeding far at sea. The only way for it to become contaminated would be through its oceanic food chain. If DDT residues are in the ocean, the tissues of this petrel are a logical place to find them, since the bird is a top carnivore; it feeds on various small cephalopods (squid).

The Bermuda petrel, incidentally, was extremely abundant about 1600. Its population was decimated by various mammals that landed with shipwrecks: rats, cats, goats, and people all liked to eat petrels. By 1630 the bird was believed to be extinct. More than 300 years later, in 1951, a small colony was rediscovered on several islets off Bermuda by Robert Cushman Murphy of the American Museum of Natural History, Wingate, and a few other ornithologists. Less than 100 individuals of the species survive. Our data go back to 1958 and represent essentially the entire world population.

The rate of reproduction—the percentage of birds that have been able to raise a chick—has been declining since 1958. Statistical analysis shows a declining regression, reaching zero reproduction in 1978. This time the bird may really be headed for extinction.

Analyses of dead chicks and eggs disclosed 6.4 ppm of DDT and its metabolites. This figure does not tell us whether or not DDT is causing the reproductive difficulties; there may be a relationship, but the DDT content is not direct evidence, and the reproductive failure could be entirely coincidental. The data do say very clearly, however, that there *is* DDT in the ocean, that it is moving through marine food chains, and that a surprising amount is present. Six ppm is not far from what we find in ospreys, eagles, peregrine falcons, and other birds that are much closer to sites of DDT application. Even ospreys that feed from sprayed marshes are only somewhat more contaminated than the Bermuda petrel.

The conclusion that there is quite a bit of DDT already in the ocean and that it is accumulating there might be a little hasty if it were based merely on a handful of analyses of the Bermuda petrel. Since the time of those tests, however, many other analyses of both fish and birds have been done from the Atlantic and the Pacific oceans, particularly from the latter. The conclusion is supported by all the analyses. Some of the shearwaters, especially from the Pacific, are more contaminated than the Bermuda petrel; these oceanic birds sometimes contain up to thirty-two ppm of DDT. Clearly DDT residues have invaded the oceans.

This problem of declining avian reproduction deserves greater detail because it is a rather sensational science story that has taken a long time to piece together. The story goes back about fifteen years to the first indications that some birds of prey were in difficulty. The best data are on the peregrine falcon, although my comments also apply to the bald eagle, the osprey, the Cooper's hawk, the sharp-shinned hawk, more recently the brown pelican, and a rather long, growing list. Each month another species seems to join the roster.

The peregrine falcon has been exhibiting several symptoms during this population decline. There has been breakage of eggs in the nest, disappearance of eggs, or no eggs at all. Behavior appears to have changed, and nesting has been later than normal. The problems of population decline stem from reproductive failure, not from mortality of adults. Peregrine falcon populations do not show wide cycles, as do some species; to the contrary, they are known for their stability. Some records go back hundreds of years because this bird was used for the sport of falconry during the Middle Ages. Nest sites in Great Britain are recorded from the twelfth century. These populations have shown remarkable stability, rarely varying by more than 5 or 10 percent per century. Suddenly, since 1950, this species has gone into a nosedive on at least three continents. In Western Europe the decline has ranged from 60 percent to complete extinction in some areas. In North America within the last ten years the bird has become extinct as a breeding species east of the Rocky Mountains. In the Rockies and to their west the population is about 5 or 10 percent of what it was—a decline of about 90 to 95 percent.

Suddenly, in the last fifteen to twenty years, we have witnessed a catastrophic decline of the peregrine, either worldwide or at least in the north temperate zone. This spectacular phenomenon occurred without any clear explanation. Nobody was sure what was happening. The birdwatchers blamed it on pesticides; they had primarily circumstantial evidence that DDT was involved (although by about 1965 the circumstantial evidence was suggestive, to say the least). Since 1967 the whole explanation has fallen into place like a jigsaw puzzle; abundant hard evidence is finally available to tell us what caused these declines.

The unraveling of the mystery began with a paper published by David Peakall of Syracuse University (now at Cornell).[4] He divided pigeons into four groups; one group was fed ten ppm of DDT; the second got two ppm of dieldrin; the third got both DDT and dieldrin; and the fourth, which served as controls, re-

ceived clean food. Ten ppm of DDT is not much for pigeons. You
can feed them many times that, and they will live out their normal lifespan and die a natural death. At ten ppm you see no
symptoms.

Peakall fed the birds these diets for a week and then killed
them. He removed the liver, homogenized it, separated the micro-
some fraction and incubated it with radioactive testosterone—
male steroid sex hormone. At the end of thirty minutes he iso-
lated the steroid fraction and subjected it to paper chromatog-
raphy. The control birds showed a single major peak—the original
unconverted testosterone. Birds which had received DDT for a
week had the original peak plus a second one. The dieldrin birds
had the original peak plus a second, but different, peak. Those
that had been given both DDT and dieldrin had all three peaks.

Following the same procedure with different groups of birds,
but this time using progesterone (female steroid hormone),
Peakall got essentially the same results. Birds that had received
DDT in their diets showed a second peak, those with dieldrin also
had a second but different peak, while birds fed DDT and dieldrin
had all three peaks.

DDT induces the formation of enzymes in the liver that
hydroxylate steroids. The extra peaks are hydroxylated deriva-
tives, which do not have the same biological activity as the original derivative. This phenomenon of hepatic enzyme induction is
quite widespread in both mammals and birds. It was studied
extensively in mammals before 1967 and since then in some
birds. Not only is the effect general among birds and mammals,
but inducers include most of the chlorinated hydrocarbon insecticides.

For birds a particular steroid, estrogen, is of special importance.
Estrogen is a major factor in the calcium metabolism of birds.
Before a female bird lays an egg, her ovaries secrete estrogen,
causing a greater uptake of calcium from her diet. The increased
calcium is stored in the hollow parts of the skeleton (the medul-
laries). Just prior to laying, this medullary bone calcium is rapidly
transferred through the blood stream to the oviduct, where it,
along with dietary calcium, forms the eggshell. Thus the medul-

laries supply the extra calcium needed to make a normal eggshell. If a bird is contaminated with a material that increases the synthesis in the liver of enzymes that attack estrogen, this would be expected to interrupt the whole sequence of events. The theoretical prediction would be that the bird would lay eggs with improperly calcified shells.

Now let us return to the field. The thickness of peregrine eggshells for the last sixty-five years has been measured by D. A. Ratcliffe, a British ornithologist.[5] An authority on peregrines, he had noted the great rate of egg breakage in the nests of these birds. Using museum specimens, he measured eggshells back to 1905. He discovered that the thickness of peregrine eggshells had been stable until the late 1940s, around 1947, when it suddenly declined about 18 percent to a lower level, where it has remained ever since. Something happened to the thickness of those shells in the late 1940s. It also happens that in the middle or late 1940s DDT was introduced on a large scale into the world environment. The two events may or may not be related.

Another British bird called the sparrow hawk, an *Accipiter* closely related to our sharp-shinned hawk which like the peregrine falcon, preys on other birds and lies at the end of a long food chain, has also been having the same set of problems, the same symptoms, the same declining population. Ratcliffe found the same results for sparrow hawks that he had found for the peregrine falcon: in the late 1940s a decline of eggshell thickness to a new and lower level, where it has remained ever since.

By the latter part of 1967 a few people were beginning to put two and two together. One of them was Joseph J. Hickey, a University of Wisconsin ornithologist. His graduate student, Daniel W. Anderson, went to museums all over the United States to measure eggshells.[6] He has measured something like 35,000 shells since then. His computer program unravels some of these data with quite interesting results. The peregrine falcon in California, half a world away from Britain, shows the same situation, with the weight of its eggshells stable since 1890 until suddenly, since 1947, the bird has been laying eggs with thin shells—roughly 18 percent thinner than they were before.

The thinning of the eggshells simultaneously occurred in Britain and thousands of miles away in California, presumably from the same cause. As I said, the event closely followed the widespread introduction of DDT.

Anderson's eggshell studies also included the red-tailed hawk, which feeds on rodents such as squirrels and mice, all herbivores. This two-step food chain proceeds from plant to animal to bird, so we would not expect a steep buildup of DDT because there are so few links in the chain and therefore little opportunity for biological concentration to take place. Consequently, we might predict that the red-tailed hawk would not accumulate large amounts of DDT, would not lay eggs with thin shells, and would not have population or reproductive problems. It turns out that this is, indeed, the case. There has been no particular change in the thickness of its eggshells and its population is stable.

The golden eagle also feeds on herbivores: rabbits, ground squirrels, and other rodents in the West. Again a two-step food chain is involved; there has been no great buildup of DDT, nor any particular change in shell thickness and population. The same circumstances hold true for the great horned owl.

Consider the bald eagle, however. It feeds on large fish; the large fish feed on smaller fish; the smaller fish perhaps feed on yet smaller fish that feed in turn on zooplankton; the zooplankton feed on phytoplankton; and the phytoplankton absorb DDT from the water. Since this food chain contains about five steps, we should expect a steep buildup of contamination toward the top. We might expect that the bald eagle would be much more heavily contaminated than are the above three species (which it is), that it would lay eggs with thin shells (which it does—18 to 20 percent thinner since 1947), and that the population would be declining (which it is, in some places quite steeply).

The osprey has a similar story. It feeds on large fish; we might therefore expect all the same occurrences that are happening with the bald eagle. This is, in fact, the case. In some areas osprey shells are 25 percent thinner than they were before 1947, and in some areas its population is declining very rapidly. In southern

Connecticut, for example, the decline has averaged about 30 percent annually.

Finally, the peregrine falcon we have already considered. But before it became extinct east of the Rockies, it laid eggs with shells 23 percent thinner than formerly.

So far everything seems to check, but there are a couple of exceptions to these data. In one Florida county the bald eagle began laying eggs with thin shells about 1943—not in 1947—and that finding initially seemed anomalous. The explanation came with the discovery that there had been large-scale testing of DDT in that one county in Florida during World War II.

There is another exception with peregrine falcons. In the mountains of California along the coast they habitually feed on sea birds. They nest on the cliffs of the outer coast range, and go to sea to feed on petrels, alcids, and other small sea birds. The waters along the California coast, especially off southern California, are heavily contaminated with DDT residues. The fish are contaminated, the petrels are rapidly disappearing, and the brown pelican is in serious trouble. It would be logical to expect the peregrine falcon to be virtually exterminated because of the contamination of its food chain. This is, in fact, the case—except for a single nest just north of Santa Barbara, where a pair raise two or three young each year. The anomaly was resolved when Robert Risebrough, molecular biologist at the University of California (Berkeley), examined the nest and found the remains of mourning doves, which are herbivores. This particular pair of peregrines did not like to eat sea birds but, instead, flew inland to prey on the doves. In consequence, we have a two-step food chain with that pair. Because of their food preference, these two birds continue to raise their young successfully.

By now I may have given you the suggestion that DDT might have something to do with the problems of these birds. Actually, what I have described so far is circumstantial evidence; all data can be accounted for as just a strange coincidence. However, there are much tighter data that establish a direct cause-and-effect relationship. Data relating the thickness of herring gulls' eggshells with the amount of DDE in ppm inside those same eggs indicate that as the DDE concentration increases inside the eggs, the shells grow thinner. There is a statistically significant relationship, with only one chance in a thousand that the relationship is based on just an accident or random phenomenon.

The real test of a relationship is whether or not we can cause the effect under controlled conditions. This experiment has been attempted several times on various gallinaceous birds. Pheasants, quail, and chickens have proved to be resistant to DDT; this fact makes it difficult to detect the effect, and scientists were misled for a long time. More recently, however, controlled experiments using the mallard duck (an omnivore), our American sparrow hawk or kestrel, and most recently the Japanese quail (a herbivore) did produce the effect.[7] Control birds on clean food (without DDT) laid normal eggs and had normal reproductive success. Birds fed DDT or DDE in their diets laid eggs with shells 15 to 17 percent thinner than normal, and they did so at concentrations approximating those found in the natural food supply.

These experiments settle the question of a cause-and-effect relationship: DDT residues *do* cause the reproductive problems of the carnivorous birds.

Questions still remain. How widespread is this phenomenon? How many species are involved? As I have noted, it seems that each month another species appears to become involved in the DDT problem, but often we lack adequate data. I know of no data on the black-crowned night heron, for example, but this species has declined considerably, and we might well expect DDT to be involved. The gannet apparently is having difficulties on the Gaspé Peninsula. Here again is a bird in a supposedly remote area feeding on fish; residues are in the fish, and a relationship with DDT would hardly be surprising. The pelican off the coast of California has been having almost complete reproductive failure. In some of its nesting colonies the pelican lays what amount to mere omelets, with almost no shell at all.

Although I started this discussion on birds with the story of the Bermuda petrel, we have no data on the thickness of its eggshells.

We have insufficient data to establish a relationship between DDT and the reproductive problems of the Bermuda petrel. We have no prewar shells for comparison. An egg laid in 1969 by a Bermuda petrel, however, is by no means normal. Often the shell flakes off the membrane, and the chick dies before hatching. The extent or magnitude of this problem is still unknown; obviously it is very serious and involves many species of carnivorous birds on several continents.

I have made no mention of fish, but they can also have very serious reproductive problems caused by DDT. In some cases 100 percent mortality of the fry occurs. This finding has been confirmed with controlled experiments similar to those described for birds.[8] The DDT concentrations that cause the effect are frequently found in the fresh-water environment and are approached—and in some cases equaled—in the ocean.

The DDT problem clearly is extremely serious. I hope that in the near future its use will end. I hope we have learned some lessons from the DDT story and that we will not need to go through twenty-five years of research with each of our other environmental problems. We do not have that much time or environment to spare.

References

[1] R. W. Risebrough et al., "Pesticides: Transatlantic Movements in the Northeast Trades," *Science* 159 (1968), 1233-36.

[2] G. M. Woodwell, C. F. Wurster, and P. A. Isaacson, "DDT Residues in an East Coast Estuary: A Case of Biological Concentration of a Persistent Insecticide," *Science* 156 (1967), 821-24.

[3] C. F. Wurster, "DDT Reduces Photosynthesis by Marine Phytoplankton," *Science* 159 (1968), 1474-75.

[4] D. B. Peakall, "Pesticide-induced Enzyme Breakdown of Steroids in Birds," *Nature* 216 (1967), 505-506.

[5] D. A. Ratcliffe, "Decrease in Eggshell Weight in Certain Birds of Prey," *Nature* 215 (1967), 208-10.

[6] J. J. Hickey and D. W. Anderson, "Chlorinated Hydro-carbons and Eggshell Changes in Raptorial and Fish-eating Birds," *Science* 162 (1968), 271-73.

[7] J. Bitman et al., "DDT Induces a Decrease in Eggshell Calcium," *Nature* 224 (1969), 44-46; R. G. Heath, J. W. Spann, and J. F. Kreitzer, "Marked DDE Impairment of Mallard Repro-duction in Controlled Studies," *Nature* 224 (1969), 47-48; R. D. Porter and S. N. Wiemeyer, "Dieldrin and DDT: Effects on Spar-row Hawk Eggshells and Reproduction," *Science* 165 (1969), 199-200.

[8] K. J. Macek, "Reproduction in Brook Trout *(Salvelinus fontinalis)* Fed Sublethal Concentrations of DDT," *J. Fish Res. Board Can.* 25 (1968), 1787-96.

The Search for an Environmental Perspective

David Brower

I hope you already agree that the environment faces many crises. I hope you soon will agree that the crises can be averted. We must realize that growth dare no longer be confused with progress. We must recognize that we have reached the end of the line in our old addiction to closing in open spaces with new development. Instead, we must do better in the spaces that we have already closed.

I am very much worried about the burgeoning efforts to make cities ubiquitous, about the rampant feeling that GNP is more important than DNA, about the assumption that society exists to serve its economy, about the Department of Housing and Urban Development's plan to put millions of houses where there are none now, and about the Forest Products Institute scheme to get into the last wilderness forests to chop down the trees to build those houses.

Note the following opinions; they will be themes in my discussion.

Paul R. Ehrlich, Stanford University biologist, says that nothing could be more misleading to our children than our present affluent society. They will inherit a totally different world, a world in which the standards, politics, and economics of the 1960s are dead.

Richard Falk, Milbank Professor of International Law at Princeton, declares that four interconnected threats overshadow our planet: wars of mass destruction, overpopulation, pollution, and

David Brower is President of Friends of the Earth, an international politically active conservation organization, and Director of the John Muir Institute, which is devoted to environmental research and education. He served as Executive Director of the Sierra Club from 1952 to 1969. He spearheaded campaigns such as those to protect Dinosaur National Monument and the Grand Canyon, and he has authored and edited many volumes on wilderness preservation. He has received many honors, including the National Parks Association Award and the Paul Bartsch Award from the Audubon Naturalist Society of the Central Atlantic States.

the depletion of resources. The essence of the problem is to find a new formula for relating man to his environment.

Norman Cousins, Editor of *The Saturday Review,* has written: "In the last phases of the Byzantine empire people directed their thoughts and energies to everyday matters rather than to the groundswells that were to break apart their civilization." And he remarked a little farther on, "Man's world is slipping away from him."

George Wald, Nobel laureate and Harvard biochemist, in his 1969 Day of Concern speech said, "I think that what we are up against is a generation that is by no means sure that it has a future. . . . We don't ask for prosperity or security. Only for a reasonable chance to live, to work out our destiny in peace and decency. Not to go down in history as the apocalyptic generation."

According to *The New York Times,* at a recent conference on "Progress in a Living Environment" held in Aspen, Colorado, John Ehrlichman, an adviser of President Nixon, was informed by assorted scientists and experts that birth control must now become compulsory, that the government has to step in and tamper with religion and personal convictions and maybe even impose penalties on the family for every child beyond two. It is in the nature of such conferences that, despite their scientific trappings and rationalistic flavor, the coup is always near at hand. Professor Garrett Hardin, a biologist from the University of California (Santa Barbara), stepped forward to recommend that the United States set a global example by celebrating the nation's bicentennial in 1976 with the declaration of a moratorium on reproduction and come as close as possible to a zero birth rate.

"But, in fact, the United States has no population explosion whatsoever," *The National Review* commented in the voice of editor-author William F. Buckley, Jr.

I would like to say right off the bat that I will take Mr. Ehrlich and Mr. Cousins and Mr. Hardin and Mr. Wald, and you can take Mr. Buckley on this subject.

In an attempt at perspective, let me recall a Ghost Ranch conference in New Mexico early in July 1969. The conference was sponsored by very sophisticated planners and by Presbyterians, who operate Ghost Ranch. I found to my amazement that the sponsors did not really quite believe that there is an ecological crisis, an environmental crisis, at all. It was uphill work for me, a conservationist. The chief conference planner declared that nature is here for man's use; if we run out of that, we will turn to something else. The Presbyterian executive (I am a drop-out Presbyterian) called man the cocreator and had very nice things to say about that view, based on the Judeo-Christian ethic. He concluded by urging that men should walk in all humility with God, which prompted me to leave behind a note saying, "I find it hard to try to walk in all humility and demand equal billing as Creator." I left before I heard his rebuttal.

I also made a rough calculation. It might not have been quite correct, but I left that behind on a note, too. Since we were at a religious conference I thought it might be good to get the perspective of how much time man has been in existence and what he has been doing with technology and the like. I put it on a scale, equating the six biblical days of creation with the 4 billion years now estimated conservatively by geophysicists as the earth's age; the equation comes out at a ratio of 8,000 years to a second. From midnight Sunday, when creation began, through Monday and up until Tuesday noon the globe, mountains, and oceans were being formed. At noon on Tuesday life boarded this planet and expanded during all the rest of Tuesday, Wednesday, Thursday, Friday, and past noon on Saturday. Life became more diverse, more stable, more beautiful. At four o'clock on Saturday afternoon the Age of Reptiles got under way, and at 9 P.M. it was offstage; just before it left, there were redwoods.

Poet Robinson Jeffers said the pelican "remembers the cone from which the first redwood fell." That is a lot of years of pelicans. Even if we stopped using DDT today, the brown pelican is doomed, because DDT will continue to concentrate in its food chain. During 1968 in the principal brown-pelican nesting area on Anacapa Island west of Los Angeles, the entire breeding colony produced only two viable young. All the rest had eggshells so soft that they were crushed when the mothers tried to brood. So that's *it* for one of the great birds!

I like to watch pelicans. Maybe you do not care about them, but I think they are really fine. I like former National Audubon Society Vice President Charles Callison's answer to the question, "Are you for people or are you for birds?" He replied, "I'm for the people who like birds."

There is more to it than that, of course. The disappearance of a bird indicates to me that there is something wrong with the environment. I have a frightening thought in my mind that maybe we are lined up behind that pelican for a similar fate.

So on to my time scale. I will skip quickly to three minutes before midnight, when man arrived aboard this planet. A second and a half before midnight Marmes Man came into the contiguous forty-eight United States in the Snake River drainage of southeastern Washington State. At a quarter of a second before midnight a bearded, anti-establishment type started talking about peace and brotherhood, and Christianity began. The Industrial Revolution commenced one-fortieth of a second before midnight. If you have been reading the newspapers lately, or your economics textbooks, you may have gotten the idea that we can project on the basis of this fortieth of a second—that since we got away with that fortieth of a second in my time scale, we can just go on accelerating the drain of our natural resources. I think people who believe this—although they may have had a great deal of schooling and advanced beyond their sophomore year (which I did not)—are stark, raving mad. Anyway, perhaps my time scale helps to put into perspective the problems of our environmental crises.

Another game helps perspective, too, and may give us insight on why we are in such trouble. It supports my opinion that we can see the end of the road right now—destruction in about a decade, unless we turn our thoughts and our way of approach to seeking solutions for our problems.

In this second game, assume that you are driving on a highway and doubling your speed every ten seconds. From one to two miles an hour, two to four, four to eight—you don't care. Eight to sixteen—mark that sixteen, because that is the highest speed man can sustain using his own energy; but we have passed that point long since. Double again, and you are up to a horse's speed of thirty-two miles an hour. Double it again, and you attain sixty-four, the top capability of the fleet cheetah. Then double it again to 128; I think that is about the speed at which we are now driving through our last resources.

At 128 miles per hour we should be pretty intent on the road, our hands firmly on the wheel. We should feel nervous. We should be hearing sirens. We *are* nervous, and we *are* hearing sirens in the concern already voiced during these discussions, in the newspapers and magazines, on television. All these are the sirens. But still many people think we can double again and speed up to 256 miles an hour. That is really happening. We have not gone off the road yet, but that does not mean we never will. We can look back and say, "We're all right, aren't we? We're still on the road, aren't we?" It is true that we are. But if we do not take our foot off the throttle and start applying brakes, if we do not think of something else to do besides double our rate of environmental destruction, we will go off the road.

Think hard about a new perspective. Such analogies might help you to develop it.

The turnaround—that is my next key word. I got it from the same Aspen, Colorado, conference attended—according to Mr. Buckley—by "kooks"; those kooks included Murray Gell-Mann, who won the 1969 Nobel Prize in physics; a White House staff member; and some other people of prestige. I was there, too, so I would qualify as a kook.

Social worker Ted Watkins was there. He helped to get the Watts section of Los Angeles back to a rebuilding phase after its disastrous August 1965 riots. He made some interesting and informative observations. Conservation did not mean very much to him. He was not worried about conserving redwood trees; he wanted to conserve people—a good idea. I would say that an environment that saves redwood trees would also be pretty good for people.

Following the devastating Watts fires, Watkins got busy and tried to start some rebuilding. He appealed to noted philanthropist-conservationist Laurance S. Rockefeller and others, and he raised a few million dollars. He moved fire victims to the empty land under the power lines of the Los Angeles Bureau of Water and Power, and they started farming it. Since water was needed, the settlers tapped the city mains. Los Angeles officials decided not to charge for the water because the farmers were watering city property. They grew palm trees and corn and flowers, and they really got some of the outdoor experience by watching what happens, how the green earth develops. They set up some parks in Watts. They got more land nearby and made a recreation area that could easily be visited from Watts.

Watkins liked best the fact that the young people started to have smiles on their faces again. He looked at us and our concern, and he asked, "What are you people willing to sacrifice to get a slightly better distribution of the good things on this earth?"

We do need to turn around. That is what I have been trying to say in establishing the perspective. We have gone through a buffalo-tongue economy (my name for it) in which we shot buffalo from moving trains for sport and used the tongue—or nothing at all—and threw the rest away. We passed through that frontier phase, but Alaska has not yet, and I am not sure that Canada has. Garrett Hardin—another "kook"—pointed out that now we must design a spaceship economy.

There is a moral in the picture we have seen from the first successful landings on the moon: our air here on earth is not very thick, and it is not getting very good care, and our soil is an extremely thin layer. Just those two natural resources, plus a little water, make all life possible, and we are being pretty ruthless with all of them. We must realize that they add up to all there is, extremely limited resources. We must do some turning around in our attitude toward those essentials for survival.

Let me suggest the composition of some of those turnarounds whose advantages would include far greater chances for peace—peace and the population explosion are handled as one item.

The major population problem can be laid at the door of affluent white America. This country uses 60 percent of the world's resources, although it has only 6 percent of the global population;

that is a ratio of about twenty-three to one. I am informed that, based on income, 1 percent of the people in the United States use 60 percent of our national resources. Where better to start population control than with the people who are using so many of this planet's resources?

Next to our number-one problem of population is that of the number-one group of villains in energy production. We probably could work out a Parkinson's Law for them. *All the power that can be generated will be utilized.* This is what we are going ahead with. We are witnessing quite a few battles, for example, with the individuals who figure that the power requirements in the United States or any region in the country are going to double every ten years. I deny that categorically. They are not. They cannot. If we keep going to reactors to accommodate such power demands, by the year 2000 we will be using up all the free-flowing fresh water to cool the reactors' condensers. I do not think anybody will want to see that happen.

This is one part of the growth syndrome; it is one of the symptoms. Energy from coal produces strip mining, from which, if we go into oil shale, we must turn a great deal of Colorado upside down.

One aspect of oil production that troubles me is the fairly recent discovery on the North Slope of Alaska. The oil companies are going to drill a ring around the Arctic Ocean from Canada, northern Baffin Island, and the islands of the Northwest Passage, in addition to digging around what was presumably found in the North Slope at Prudhoe Bay. It is bad enough when you have an oil breakaway off Santa Barbara, California, where it may be a disguised blessing because people see what is happening. Who will see what happens in Alaska or who will care enough? Who will care about tundra, for example, if permission is given for the hot-line proposed to bring the oil 800 miles across Alaska? Who cares what will happen up there? It is all wilderness anyway. Who cares what will happen if there is some offshore drilling at Prudhoe Bay and a few oil breakaways occur? The region represents a major migration route for a large part of the Pacific fishery, which spends some of its time in that area of the Arctic Ocean.

Suppose that we had a whole fleet of giant tankers like the *Manhattan,* and one of them were wrecked, leaving 300,000 tons of oil loose somewhere up there? It would make the *Torrey Canyon* disaster off England look rather minor. What would that do to the Northwest Passage, to the Arctic ecology, which has not been studied yet? We do not know those answers.

But we have an urge to put a big free oil port at Machiasport, Maine, so that we can dock those 300,000-ton tankers. Studies on the Machiasport proposal by Keith Roberts at Harvard indicate that such a seagoing monster takes ten miles to stop once it is up to speed, and two miles to turn at that rate. I do not like that kind of maneuverability—or lack of it—off the coast of some of the most beautiful country in the United States. But that is the price for oil.

I could tell you a lot more about oil and the proposed Alaskan pipeline and why I have been testifying against it in Congress, but let's go on to another form of energy. If we do not want to use oil or fossil fuels, how about nuclear reactors? Do we really want to go ahead with them at this stage? I am quite apprehensive. Can we finally get them operating without the possible escape of tritium and radioactive krypton? What do we do when a reactor plant becomes obsolete and has to be buried? Where do we dig a hole for a tired, hot reactor? What do we do, primarily, with high-level waste?

I recently attended a convention of reactor salesmen, as I like to put it, in Chicago. The Argonne Universities Association was wondering what to do with their brain pool now that they believe the reactor problem to be just about solved. James T. Ramey, Atomic Energy Commissioner, while reading a very long speech, said that "to save time I will skip the next few pages." Those three pages discussed high-level wastes; I read them and found that he did not give a very good summary of them. He labeled critics of reactors as part of the "hogwash syndrome," which I will join. He talked about their objections to a proposal to con- centrate radioactive waste, encase it in glass, and put it in a salt mine on the assumption that a salt mine neither contains nor is likely to contain water; if the canisters should break or something else should expose the waste, radioactivity would supposedly not be escaping into the ecosystem.

Maybe that is a fine idea, but nobody is carrying it out. Instead, I am quite reliably informed, wastes are still taken from San Onofre in southern California, put into concrete, and dumped into the ocean. The authorities are still trying to handle wastes at the Hanford atomic works in Washington State in stainless-steel tanks. They think that about every fifteen years the wastes must be removed by remote control to new tanks because of the old ones' deterioration. They believe that this process will have to continue for a thousand years. I do not think we have done *anything* very well for a thousand years except multiply.

I am worried quite a bit, too, about the engineers, the people who like to build dams. I have always equated the U.S. Bureau of Reclamation and Army Corps of Engineers with beavers because they cannot stand the sight of running water. They still try to use old answers for new problems. I believe we really have run out of dam sites and must do something else besides enlarging water supplies, increasing power generation, and expanding our artificial lake playgrounds.

I am worried about the people masquerading as foresters who are actually timber engineers. (I do not mind attacking foresters, even when I am sponsored by them. I am sponsored in part in the John Muir Institute by Robert O. Anderson, Chairman of the Board of Atlantic Richfield, and I attack their oil pipelines, too.) Foresters worry me because they are too concerned about getting the wood out. They are trying to counterattack against conservation gains of recent years and are threatening our remaining wild forests.

Now I must mention my worry about the road gang, which is essentially Detroit, and the freeways that Detroit requires to carry new and bigger cars.

My concern is not just for the pollutants we know about, but for the pollutants—as Rockefeller University biologist René Dubos points out—that we do not know about. It took us a long time—fifty-seven years—to identify radiation as a hazard to man. How well are we measuring many of the materials responsible for air pollution?

Polychlorinated biphenyls, a byproduct of the plastics industry, have permeated the global ecosystem and are as bad as DDT. They have been produced for quite a while, but we just learned recently that they are a major, far-spreading, dangerous pollutant. That threat, plus whatever else may be leaking out of the same industrial process, worries me and Dubos; it has led Max Linn, President of the John Muir Institute, to suggest that we find a substitute for plastics.

The energy boys, the engineers, the road gang, the people who pave more and more highways, the people who dig up more oil and make sure we spend it faster and put it into the atmosphere faster, all are prominent among today's villains.

In effect, the road gang is taking years out of our lives because of the impairment of our environment. It is pretty bad when Los Angeles needs a smog alert to warn parents against allowing their children to take part in any major exercise; those are the days when the air is actually visible and we can smell it. What about the constant impairment of our health? What about the reports of pollutants that are kept out of smokestacks in the daytime but are emitted at night, when we are not as likely to notice them? We are getting some infrared checks, I understand, on various manufacturing areas to see who is doing that, but it is bad news for us all.

I have just declared them all villains and could name many more.

But in fairness I must refer to cartoonist Walt Kelly's "Pogo." If you have read your Pogo well, you know he says that finally, somewhere, "with small flags waving and tinny blasts on tiny trumpets we shall meet the enemy, and not only may he be ours. He may be us."

That is where the *real* enemy is, in case you were wondering. It is each of us. We buy the cars that burn too much fuel and that spew particulate rubber into the air when we hit the corners or accelerate too fast, and we spew particulate asbestos into the air when we hit the brakes. Both of these pollutants are carcinogenic (capable of producing cancer). This is not to mention all the other pollutants caused by cars.

Suppose you do not buy the car that pollutes our environment. Suppose you cut your car size in half; or if you have a small car, you get a motorcycle; or if you have a motorcycle, you get a bicycle; or if you have a bicycle, you walk. Suppose you step down and make the air work a little bit better for yourself and everybody else. Who is willing to do that? If you are not willing to leave those monsters in the showroom—a very corrective action, I think, because Detroit would come around pretty fast—then you are guilty.

Do not let me try to act as if I were not equally at fault. All by myself I drive an old beat-up car across the San Francisco Bay Bridge every day, using up all that highway, all that gasoline, when I should be taking the mass transportation we soon will have to accept as essential to antipollution.

We need rapid solutions like the proposal by Dan Luten of the University of California (Berkeley) for mass transportation, for toll highways or toll bridges; he suggests that cars be charged on the Bay Bridge for empty seats. Under Luten's plan, if you are driving a full car, you go free; if you go with five seats empty, you are charged $2. This is a quick solution. Why not try it on our freeways, our superhighways?

You are a villain if, knowing what you know, you refuse to share your apple with a worm. If you insist on enjoying your apple wormfree, you will also have the not-visible DDT on the apple and in the atmosphere—and if not DDT, its various successors, which are a far larger part of the persistent-chlorinated-hydrocarbon business than is DDT itself, which is down to about .01 percent. Do not be fooled if the restriction of DDT fails to abolish the real problem. You are a villain, therefore, if you insist on having DDT spread on everything to assure a neater crop for you to eat. Bite a worm sometime; it will not hurt you nearly so much as DDT does.

There are other solutions for the pesticide problem: to stop trying to design crops to fit the machine, to design them to fit the land and ecosystem, and to use the natural diversity of living things as one of the elements that carried them on through—all the way through from midnight last Tuesday, if you remember.

There are many other examples that identify ourselves as the villains. We are villains if we keep collecting things. I already have too much stuff at home, but I keep on buying things I do not need. As a species we habitually buy things that are a perpetual drain on the rapidly emptying resource base. We buy cars; we disperse them around the landscape eventually. We buy beer cans; they are everywhere and not recoverable under our wasteful system. As birth control advocate Stephanie Mills has put it, we are all good Nazis in the war against the planet. I think we had better change our ways.

There are a few ways to try. We must think more about using our own ingenuity. We must think about looping the system more often, recycling, doing more with less.

If you have heard inventor R. Buckminster Fuller talk about birds' eggs and their structuring, and have really explored designing with nature, as urban architect Ian McHarg does, you know how beautiful an egg is. An egg has good design in the process by which it is laid. An airborne bird could not carry a full clutch of eggs; the system has been worked out so that a mother bird will be able to lay one egg at a time, and at the end of the right time, with the correct number of eggs, she adds the magic element—consecutive heat. With the emergence of the chick, the yolk, the white, all have become blood and beak and feathers. It is all there in a pretty, neat system. Nothing was added and nothing was taken away from that egg.

That is a model on which we should pattern more of our own work. That is the challenge for technology. Do it well or approach it well.

There are other things to do, too. You might even join an organization or two or three or four, and make a small investment in your environment. A new one with a fairly good purpose is the John Muir Institute, intended primarily for research and conferences and for getting authors and photographers together to publish books. The research is in areas that are not covered now.

I have several categories of such major research vacuums.

For example, we need an independent check of big projects that are going to have a major effect on the environment. My biggest fight with Stewart Udall erupted when his Department of the Interior initiated a project that I thought was going to bother the environment; the department's Bureau of Reclamation wanted dams in the Grand Canyon, and we very much did not. The Bureau of Reclamation could not be expected to conduct a very objective study of its program and it did not, in my opinion.

On the other hand, the Interior Department did carry on a good study—maybe not as objective as it should have been—on the proposed Rampart Dam on the Yukon River in Alaska. A good study was made by Stephen Spurr of the University of Michigan, who brought in independent experts from all over the country. For about $40,000 a four-volume report was published on the Rampart Dam that, together with the Fish and Wildlife Services' adverse findings, discredited the project. At least the plan was abandoned for the time being. Interior Secretary Walter J. Hickel was a supporter of the Rampart Dam plan when he was Governor of Alaska, so I do not relax now.

We also need a system for checking to see if promises are carried out in the operation of a project. The Missouri Valley project is being reviewed by Carlos Stern, a South African graduate student at Cornell. He has examined it in detail and discovered that the differences are amazing between the promises and what was delivered. We need more such independent research. The imminence of such critiques would correct a tendency to overpromise on such projects.

We need research on the rates of recovery of the environment. If our civilization commits acts from which our environment can hardly recover, we had better set up some strong limitations. We would be wise to concentrate on doing things that permit our environment to bounce back quickly.

We need, somehow, to set up a commission on fair conservation practices in manufacturing, and we must give the public a chance to make its viewpoint obvious by purchasing from people who use good conservation practices and by not buying from the others. That would produce a rapid change in the habits of manufacturers.

We need to find out how to get careers in conservation built into everybody—not a career in conservation, but a *conscience for conservation* built into everybody's career, whether he is a banker or an economist or an anthropologist.

Take anthropologists as an example. If we are ever going to live again in equilibrium with our environment, we need the best possible information about who lived in equilibrium in the past.

A banker should be capable of going right at the language of the FHA requirement that to qualify for a loan a site must be level. An incredible amount of land has been destroyed because of ignorance implicit in that simple clause! Senator Russell Long (D-Louisiana) almost lost us even more, but fortunately the Senate Finance Committee did not go along with his idea. He wanted to put a capital-gains tax on inherited property. Think about that one for a moment. Imagine that your grandfather paid $10 an acre for 1000 acres of land, but now it is worth $1000 an acre and you inherit it. Under the Long proposal, you would have to pay a capital-gains tax on that inheritance. You might have to put it on the market in distress. It would be bought up and possibly subdivided—another great big piece of open space gone. It could happen again and again in just that way. Fortunately, the Senate prevented such an eventuality.

Finally, we need (and soon) a series of meetings on the economics of peaceful stability. If we believe the evidence sent back from the Apollo moon flights and the photographs of our spaceship Earth, we should work for a spaceship economy. John Maynard Keynes did not have that idea in mind; rather, he visualized a limitless economy and limitless resources. How do we restructure our economy to accommodate the knowledge that there is only our one planet, one store of resources, and no more thereafter? It is not a comfortable idea to consider. It is new thinking, but why not try it?

Garrett Hardin tells of a man 300 years ago who looked down and suddenly realized that his left foot was different from his right. Before that simple discovery there had been only one kind of shoe, which fit either foot. But from then on cobblers made left and right shoes. Thirty years later, the British army got the idea. The point: there is still time for a little insight now.

If corporations and you will believe that we can get by without a constant expansion of the economy, you will be willing to see that expansion end. If you infer that without expansion you are dead, you will keep on expanding until you die—indeed, because you will have run out of resources.

Those are the kinds of research we are trying to carry on at the John Muir Institute.

Friends of the Earth, meanwhile, is trying to provide this kind of information to conservation organizations as ammunition for all their battles in legislative halls and the political arena. That effort is new in the field of conservation: going all out to be substantial lobbyists. The organization is going to try to enter into the decision-making phase in contests between candidates for public office. Never again, I hope, will we have a presidential election campaign in which our environment is totally dismissed as an issue. I think it has been in the past.

All these actions on behalf of our environment can be taken. The main problem is to motivate individuals. We have every reason to abandon our former goals of an ever-expanding, ever-growing economy. We need, not an expanding economy, but an expanding individual, said the late Howard Gossage, one of the best advertising men. I believe we can achieve that goal. I believe we can make the plan work. I believe we can live on a 90 percent earth (assuming 10 percent to be the part of our planet that man has not messed up already).

If only 10 percent really is all that we have left, let's stop right now wherever wildness exists and not harm it any more. Let's turn around. Let's go back over the 90 percent we already have touched—sometimes well, too often not well, in our cities and our farms, wherever man has laid his hands. Let's go back and do better. That last 10 percent cannot possibly stand against our continuing destruction of resources. If we think that it will and we go right on to the uttermost brink, we must get ready to fall off. When we get to that brink, we will have to turn around and claw our way back, using our ingenuity, our technology, our science, our humaneness if we are to remain here at all.

Why not stop now and leave something here that will keep some of the world beautiful? Why must we careen to a cliff of repugnance before we stop? Why can't we leave the earth's wildness, for the answers it holds to questions man has not yet learned how to ask?

As Ignazio Silone, an Italian novelist of the 1930s, put it, "The only true dignity of man is his ability to continue to fight against insurmountable odds."

That may be too serious. Try Pogo: "We're confronted with insurmountable opportunities."

A Strategy for the Ghetto:
The Philadelphia Story

Harold J. Haskins

I am a community organizer. I have worked in the community—Philadelphia—for at least fifteen years. One of my prime discoveries is that some basic and sound elements in institutions within the ghetto community, the black community, still have not been destroyed. One of those institutions happens to be the teenage gang. I am very much interested in this type of group.

When I first came out of Penn State and Temple universities, I became involved in working on street corners. For thirteen years I worked on street corners with gangs to try to determine the problems of the system as the gang saw them. I have to admit that we did not get very far. There were few solutions that we could muster other than maintenance, other than helping these young fellows to get past the action of the night or possibly keep from being shot or from being placed in an institution or jail.

Actually I got some insight by looking at their community through the eyes of the gang members, looking at it from the perspective of a young fellow who probably had not been across town (even if he were thirteen or fourteen or fifteen years of age) because of gang boundaries. As I became more interested and more involved, I saw also that these young guys had lots of problems that could have been relieved if right then we could have supplied some fundamental solutions, such as self-sufficiency, self-determination, and the other "self" values that people talk about and have been talking about all during the 1960s.

The 12th & Oxford Streets gang lives in a model-cities district

Harold J. Haskins is Director of Community Development of the Temple University Health Sciences Center. He is guiding the evolution of a Community Development Corporation and a corresponding workshop to serve 35,000 northern Philadelphia residents. He drew national attention for directing the hostile teenage 12th & Oxford Streets gang toward the filming of 'The Jungle,' a successful movie of their own world, which gave them insight, human identity, motivation, and social acceptance. He has been a consultant on ghetto problems for several federal agencies.

in North Philadelphia. This district is one-third of the area of Philadelphia. As usual, the area is unworkable—it is too big. There are no institutions, few programs that can be of assistance to the people of this community. There is no viable community-partici- pation program because the governmental structure in Philadel- phia has made the citizens-participation unit a rubber-stamp com- mittee that approves programs developed downtown. But a few groups, including the 12th & Oxford Streets gang, have begun trying to do something, even though they cannot articulate the problems of our society and do not have much knowledge about the basis of the problems in the system.

Their deficiency might sound like ignorance. It may sound like stupidity. But how different are these young men from middle- class America? A group of young fellows, who for once do not have the police on their backs, who do not have their old prob- lems with other gangs, are viewing their turfs, their communities, their neighborhoods as places where they can do something to help themselves.

I contacted the 12th & Oxford Streets group in 1966. I had some money to make a film. I knew nothing about film making, but I believed that if I could gain their attention, hire them, find them some kind of training program, involve them in that pro- gram so that they could really learn some basic skills of film making, they would probably have fewer problems with the law for maybe the next two months. That is how we got involved in this experience.

I hired a cameraman. I hired a secretary and the war lords, the gang leader, the council, and at least twenty-five young men who were the hierarchy of the 12th & Oxford Streets group (which has approximately 400 members).

I said to them, "I want you guys to get involved in the experi- ence of making a film."

They laughed, and they drank wine; they played cards, and they laughed again. And I laughed. But I went back again, and we finally got into it when one of the guys said, "Yes, let's try it."

We set up classes in a place called Heritage House at Broad and

Master Streets in Philadelphia—right in their neighborhood—and got ready to shoot the movie.

That film, "The Jungle," was made by a teenage gang of high-school dropouts. It tells their own story—the tale of a group of young men who live in North Philadelphia. The guys show fights; they show dances; and they show wine drinking. They show one vitally important fact: that for the first time outside of their own normal way of life they were working together toward a goal, producing something.

The experiences they encountered in producing "The Jungle" were tremendous. (The police in two instances locked up the entire film crew.) The really important result was that these young men had been involved in a new experience.

After the film was made in 1967, we had twenty-two minutes of film, no money, and now 400 guys. My home is right in the neighborhood, the turf. In living there, I experienced the situation every day. We looked at ourselves and asked, what do we do next? I had to find methods and programs.

This is the story. I want to tell you the story of "The Jungle" so that you will see the developmental sequence in which these young men became involved in a situation that, because of sheer numbers, prevented film making from being the only experience. After all, how many movie companies could we have?

"Who wants to be part of a movie company?" I asked. "All of you who want to be a movie company stand over here."

About twelve guys stood over to the left.

Now how many guys did I have left in the playground? About 388.

"Well, what else do you want to do?"

One of them said, "Look, you know I have been thinking about these guys who come around here every Saturday morning and collect eighteen dollars rent from my mother. Landlords—we can be one of them." Just like that.

I said, "Really?"

"Well," he went on, "if they can collect rent and don't fix up the house, we can get some loans and put up some new buildings, and maybe, you know, have the houses too. We can own them, right?"

That's fine. Okay, what's next?

Another guy said, "You know that woman down the street? She has two laundry machines and both of them broke. My mother could never, never come to that place and get her laundry cleaned. We'd like to have a laundromat."

Okay. Let's think about that.

Someone else said, "I'm interested in fixing up houses."

Let's think about that, too.

We ended up with several different ideas and with several groups of young men who became interested in enterprise or development programs for their own neighborhood. After they became exposed, their plan was to go out to the schools, to the government, to wherever you have to go, and make money off that film. We had no money.

The boys were to report back to the council meetings and tell us what they observed. That was a very important point; we put that rule into operation on purpose. They reported everything. In one instance a guy took a plane trip. He wanted wine, but he was afraid to ask. He ordered a martini instead and was sick all the way to California.

"Don't change your habits," I told him. "Be what you are; do what you have to do. If you don't have wine, don't get anything."

That's the issue.

Exposure came to these young men quickly. They met people of many social strata and of different religions and ethnic groups; they found out that such intermingling can be rewarding. Several gang members reported that the audiences asked "the same damn questions." All over the place they ask the same questions, in their colleges, universities, churches, other places: "Don't you guys want two and a half kids with a two and three-quarter garage out in the suburbs next to me?" The people who asked those questions were white.

The boys always replied, "I don't want to live next to you in the suburbs. Who wants to travel back and forth from town all the time?" Then they would add, "We'd rather fix up our own turf, if you don't mind."

Another effort I made with the young members of the group was to give them or find them jobs that were relevant to the areas in which they were interested. For instance, some guys wanted to be involved in housing; we found them jobs in the Philadelphia Housing Development Corporation as housing inspectors. They learned the required skills very well without a high-school education.

Other members of the group who were interested in handling the funds of the corporation became involved and interested in banking as a career. With a little manipulation we placed some fellows in Philadelphia banks. They are doing very well now. They are going back to school, too. Some were trained by Price Waterhouse, an accounting firm, to learn basic accounting and bookkeeping. These members were plugged in one-to-one to bookkeeper and accountant-type persons to handle the 12th & Oxford Streets gang's books.

After that, several young men were employed by the Philadelphia Gas Works to learn preventive maintenance on gas dryers. This training program was in preparation for a laundromat business.

What we really are saying is that ours is a small effort. We are talking about a piece of an action, not about the whole big universe. We are not talking about a whole world. We are not talking about the whole environment of the country.

We are talking about the environment of a turf of approximately fifteen to twenty square blocks in north central Philadelphia, smack in the middle of the model-cities community. A group of young men now own twenty-some houses there. Several of them are in college, because they knew they had to get an education to maintain their own enterprises. Several are running various businesses. Others have found some mechanism to go back to school through various grants that we have received.

This was just a gang, a natural group. It took me thirteen years of hard labor to find a solution to the problem of how to keep one gang from fighting another gang or how to keep them from having any need to join in gang wars. Now they have become interested in convincing other groups to form enterprises.

We can talk about black economic development; that is one thing. But the real issue is that every piece of the program in which these young men are involved relates to community development as they contribute it to their own turf. It is small, but it is something. When you are dealing on a one-to-one basis in an everyday situation all of the time, when you get to the point where you are just performing a maintenance function of relieving everyday problems as they occur and you do not see an end, you can go crazy.

It is all a sad story when someone tells what does happen while working on the everyday maintenance function. But when you know that there is something going on like the 12th & Oxford Film Makers Corporation (as they are now called)—which has influenced several other gang groups to form corporations in North Philadelphia—then there is hope.

Yet they are not aware of all the problems in our society today. It is interesting to note how many people in this country, especially in the urban communities, are not really aware of the problems, beyond the fact that asthma, emphysema, and other diseases are knocking us off all the time.

The gang found that out and at the same time made another discovery: planning can be a hustle, and it is a hustle on the part of the white establishment. It is a piece of the action that the establishment uses to do what it wants to do—move a building here, move somebody out there—like playing Monopoly, and some people play Monopoly in the Planning Commission. They don't even care about money. They just get drawings together, and they do crazy things they term environmental design or urban design or whatever they decide to call it.

Our guys went to the officials and asked, "How come you moved that building over there? That's my mother's house. I'll beat you. I'll punch you in the mouth; you know what I mean?" Wow, after that! That really happened, because it was a situation where a block was cleared out, and one guy's house was right there. When he checked it out and went back into the community, he said, "Hey, Mom; they're going to move this place out of here, you know?"

Somehow the perspective came from top to bottom that young men could become involved in the planning process. The guys got actively involved in the 12th & Oxford Streets program from a community-planning aspect as well as from the perspective of the Environmental Planning Department, a division of the Philadelphia Planning Commission. What came out of all that? They have made their base map drawings and have set up their programs.

Such is the basis of the whole concept of grass-roots planning that we are developing currently. What we are trying to do is simply to bring home to individuals that if they get involved in a block-by-block program for their community, have everything documented in a planning process, and also use political muscle to flaunt the plans in front of a committeeman or ward leader, they have a better chance of getting some real action. They may have a better chance of getting a piece of the capital budget brought to their community. What we are suggesting is to take it from that grass-roots (or 12th & Oxford Streets) point of view.

We can project those ideas to the whole concept of community development on a larger scale. We can do it by using institutions as a piece of the action; by using prospective developmental projects such as the nation's 1976 Bicentennial as a piece of the action; by using whatever we can latch onto to help change the environment, which is deteriorating rapidly in certain sections of the ghetto in Philadelphia.

We are simply saying that there are vast chances for improvements once a community becomes sophisticated in using specialists correctly, once it has been taught to ask the proper questions. Ask the proper questions, and we make waves in the black community. We change certain aspects of it. These changes are happening now.

Take the 12th & Oxford Streets gang—which has become the 12th & Oxford Film Makers Corporation since the success of the film, "The Jungle." We asked them the right questions, made waves, and they took it from there. They scored a major achievement, formed a corporation as a result, and kicked me out in January 1969. They had become self-sufficient. They have their own program. They have gotten grants from the federal government and are doing very well.

In January 1969 I left 12th & Oxford Streets and began working with a community called the Tioga-Nicetown Area. I wanted to expand on this idea of turf and a community. We became involved in the concept of a community-development program that would require bringing together experts, consultants, architects, proposal writers, health planners, and various other specialists to a specific physical location in a large urban center. We worked at the Temple Health Sciences Center, to which the Tioga Community was immediately adjacent.

We gathered together the Citizens of Tioga-Nicetown (COT-N) —an umbrella organization of twenty-three or more groups—mainly for information and communications purposes. The group meets every two weeks for discussion of problems experienced by each person, each group, or each block. At the same time we were building a community-planning workshop that originally had a few specialists in city planning. Since that time several other types of experts have become directly involved.

This is our concept of the workshop. The COT-N group has task forces in housing, education, recreation, youth development, human services, and employment. Each task force has a chairman, who relates to the corresponding specialists in the workshop on a one-to-one basis for developing programs for action. Our specific objective is to pull together, block by block, the ideas and program interests of the 130-block Tioga area, a community that is fast deteriorating but is not yet dead, as is the model-cities district.

We feel that the whole environmental situation there justifies this kind of planning effort. With grants for specific projects, three of which have been identified, and some initial funding still forthcoming, we expect to get the planning momentum rolling in this community. We are starting a political-awareness workshop, too. We hope that this political muscle and the planning muscle and all our other efforts from the grass roots up will affect in some measure the whole idea of the urban community and the zone of transition in the ghetto.

Why are we taking all those actions? Not because we have solid hopes of any kind, but simply because there is nothing else to do. If we think about the frustrations that we endure today, we have to do what we know best.

So what do we ask? What do we bring into Tioga? We ask people to come in who have skills. We want people who are interested in contributing or selling their time if we have the money for those specific skills that we need. We will articulate what those skills will be.

We do not want any superliberals and people with a rescue fantasy. We do not want people who walk around with their personality on their hips—that is, offering services to our community only because of their own need or guilt. We do not want the problems of the white society. All we want are skills. We will take those skills; we will ask the proper questions and put them to work.

My role as Director of Community Development at Temple University is very precarious. Let's face it; I'm stoned. Excuse my expression; that's slang for anti-institution. But I am working for an institution. I am saying to the institution, frankly and partly because of the institution's own dilemmas about expansion, that if we have a strong community group, we do not have to go around asking, "Where is the community?"

If we allow a community group to develop, at least it will be in a position to negotiate or to do whatever else is necessary, rather than burn down houses. We know the power of the institution, of Temple, of the city—but the real issue is that the Tioga community now is incorporating institutional inputs.

There are three categories of organizations for the Citizens of Tioga-Nicetown: the community umbrella group, the churches (six are involved), and educational institutions and Tioga schools (as well as the Temple University Health Sciences Center). The organization is currently negotiating with industries along its borders to add possibly a fourth category for program supports. Two of these industries are the Budd and

Tasty Cake Companies. We are "turning on" everybody in Tioga now.

We are finding out that there is a lot of power in this organization. We have not assessed all of the power that is there. The ladies who participated in the old poverty program years ago have become quite active in COT-N. Three teenage gangs in the community are interested and working on the youth-development task force.

Now what is the role of an educational institution such as Temple—or Yale? Believe me, so many resources can be mustered from educational institutions of that size that can change the face of a community and environment. We need not talk about those resources; educational institutions are big business. We must solve problems by trying to convince administrators in these institutions of their responsibilities to the surrounding community.

The educational institution is not cranking out a program to help people in the community to produce change. It has to send resources and community-organization people out to make things happen. This is very important. You cannot just teach craftsmanship or physical-development packaging or the other skills necessary for a community to realize self-sufficiency; you must program in a concrete community-development agenda.

We are not playing games any more. The first game was the poverty program, the second game was model cities. The community is wise to these games; the community is coming back with planning approaches. Legal negotiations are now the community counterplay to support communities to approach and attain self-sufficiency. We have defined community *self-sufficiency* as that aspect of development that permits an area to build in permanent change. The university should be responsible to provide program supports for new housing, education, and job programs. All these aspects should fit into program packages—*community-development packages.*

Communities are tired of seeing the foundations and other philanthropic organizations give big grants to research projects. They are tired of seeing programs taken over by professors for whatever research needs or controls they want personally.

In Tioga we are talking about skills, skills in our turf. We can submit to you a proposal from our workshop—crank out one right away with all the plans for a specific problem in Tioga. We can give you a cost estimate of how much money it is going to take to run such a project—all this coming from a community organization.

The real problem is that urban educational institutions can be accused rightly of hustling their own programs. They are hustling urban-design monies, planning monies, project-and-research monies that communities could use.

Somebody walked over to one of Temple Health Sciences Center's new buildings and put up a sign reading, "Let's rebuild Tioga now." Buttons of all dimensions proclaim that sentiment on many coats and sweaters in North Philadelphia.

I am not pessimistic at all. The mix in skills in that 130-block area is diffuse enough. With these skills we are developing recognition from the city, from Temple, and so on. Compared to the 12th & Oxford Streets area, this community has high home ownership, possibly 50 to 60 percent. It has a good chance to win the war on blight.

My role in community development places me squarely on the fence at times. I am suspect to the community at times. I am suspect to the institutions. Frankly, that is of no consequence if we are able to build in the concept of community development. This concept has been expanded from a gang community-development philosophy to a group concept of communities, organizations, and institutions. We are pulling notions and hopes together. We are establishing a process to implement several projects in Tioga to abate the deterioration problem. Housing has deteriorated rapidly in the last ten years. Slum landlords and land speculators abound. This is the pattern: whoever controls the land, whoever owns the houses, can easily dictate political authority.

COT-N is attacking this problem by buying up houses, establishing a code enforcement program, and developing a land-bank program. My main task now is to solicit funds for Tioga for the planning workshop. We are talking to large foundations about grants for the community organization. We are talking to the institution about charging less overhead on grants that would go out into the community.

People like myself and others can define the targets, and we are defining them. The big problem is the people who will help us lay the foundation to implement programs. If this concept succeeds, it will be much easier for other communities, with assistance from the university and other resources, to redevelop large areas of the city. Universities have to deliver programs to communities that those communities handle and control themselves; self-sufficiency is based on the administrative bits and pieces that the community controls.

Suppose a community organization learns how to "hire" and use Price Waterhouse or Arthur D. Little Consultants or one of the large architectural firms for projects budgeted to the neighborhood. In Tioga now we have identified projects that will deliver certain incentives—"trade-offs"—to industry and developers. We have learned how to attract the established firms to generate financial support for the area. Fairly soon we may even have community participation through community trust funds and holding companies. It is a fairly easy process once it gets rolling.

Universities have a strange habit of sending out community-oriented but university-based programs. Most of these programs are shooting for the mass and are fragmented or duplicate services. Health programs are a good example: they do not have cross-references or "bridges" with each other.

One wonders if academic freedom is the license for deterioration of community. The more that people see separated programs coming into the community without concentration and co-ordination, the more they realize that they are being separated from their neighborhoods.

I guess this is the problem with the whole concept of academia. Each department head and researcher must have *his* project, directly intended for *his* target population. He must have his staff and all his administrative autonomy. There is no need for such waste of money on research unless that research demonstration spins off permanent development in the target area. Where in this country is this happening? Most universities are guilty of program disjointedness.

COT-N has found a way to bring institutional programs together to share data. COT-N is developing through its workshop a data-collection center to deal with "community"-oriented programs in the university. We hope this effort will prepare the way for joint community-university proposals. This is an example of a community group's giving information to an institution.

I do not know much about the whole concept of academia, except that I hate to see it hustle money the way it has been doing throughout this country. So far as man and his environment are concerned, I do not understand why institutions such as Yale fail to make significant contributions in a realistic and moral sense to the urban problem. It should be pretty damn easy if one evaluates available resources.

If we can just get certain people off of their own "self-interest" and onto the use of their skills for the development of a neighborhood—then man's environment may look a little better for him and his neighbors.

Congress and Environmental Quality: Now or Never

Paul N. McCloskey, Jr.

Consider some of the historical perspectives by which we have reached today's crisis in our environment. Compare these perspectives with some of the legal aspects in our national institutions, our cultural heritage, and our traditions against which we will seek in the decade ahead to solve our environmental problems. If our institutions are to attack these problems successfully, it is important to view them against their historical perspectives.

First, the evolution of our own law. Since the first colonists landed in this country from England, almost every law that has been enacted at any governmental level has been designed to encourage and assist the development of land, the promotion of commerce, the utilization of natural resources, and the working of our land to increase the standard of living. Now public opinion demands that conservation, preservation, and rehabilitation of the environment have a higher priority than development. If we are to reverse the process of history, therefore, we must recognize that most of this nation's laws, built up over nearly 190 years, are out of date; they will have to be changed, tinkered with, and modified if the new goal of conservation is to prevail.

Second, the evolution of tax laws and tax structure in our federal system. I am confident that air and water pollution, the disposal of solid wastes, and the reduction of jet noise are simple problems that we can see and deal with by assigning technology and money to their solution. The graver problems are aspects of our institutions that have an *indirect* impact on the environment.

Paul N. McCloskey, Jr., is U.S. Representative for the 11th District of California (San Mateo County). He has served on several congressional committees dealing with conservation and natural resources and on the Republican Task Force on Population and Earth Resources. A former president of the Palo Alto Area Bar Association and the Conference of Barristers of the State Bar of California, he was a delegate to the White House Conference on Civil Rights in 1963. He has been active in a number of conservation organizations.

Traditionally in this country we have treasured the prerogatives of local government; we have believed that the more institutions we could govern locally, the better—from our educational system to our municipal government. We have based the financing of local government almost entirely on the local property tax. This procedure was fine when rich and poor people lived in the same city, where the rich man's property was more highly taxed so that the poor man's children could get the same education, could have the same benefits of urban living. But today our zoning laws, the growth of affluence, the flight from the cities have all caused the erection of an entirely different structure. Rich people live in one city, which may have one-acre, two-acre, or even five-acre zoning. Middle-income people may live in an entirely different city, which has a different level of income and a different property-tax base. Poor people live either in the rural regions or in the ghetto areas of the major cities. There is a growing disparity between rich and poor, particularly in education.

In my own San Mateo County, south of San Francisco, one of the most affluent counties in the nation, some school districts spend $910 annually for the education of each child because the property-tax base in their particular cities supports that level of education, with topflight teachers, ideal classroom sizes, small classes, and the best of teaching assistance. In other areas of my county only $500 is spent each year per child. Thus, the black children and poor white children today grow up in areas where the property tax determines that they get less of an education than that available to the youngsters of wealthy people.

That disparity in education makes a myth of the proud claim of equal opportunity in this nation, because equal opportunity requires an equal educational opportunity. In a black high school of my district young people are graduating with a seventh-grade reading level. Of course they cannot compete for admission to college.

I use that example because it is at the bottom of our fight against the poor quality of our environment. If we want local government to cope with air pollution, water pollution, and disposal of wastes, today we ask the poorest of our governmental levels to take away from its skimpy property-tax resources money that is presently required for education and welfare.

Compare the local government and its tax base with the state tax picture. We used to try to equalize local education and welfare expenditures by state contributions. Today state governments generally draw their primary revenues from such sources as sales taxes, use taxes, gas taxes, lotteries, horse race taxes, liquor excise taxes—a whole collection of items that fall between local property taxes and federal income taxes.

Finally, there is the United States government, the recipient of perhaps the only nonregressive tax in this country: the federal income tax. Why? Because in 1913, when we adopted the sixteenth Amendment to the U.S. Constitution to permit the graduated income tax, that money went to the federal government.

The growth of federal revenues is primarily attributable to four wars: World Wars I and II, the Korean War, and the Vietnam conflict. It is possible to trace both our national debt of $365 billion and the fact that the federal government gets most of the usable tax revenues to the circumstance that, after the wars requiring high tax revenues, those revenues have continued to pour in at an increasing rate, particularly since the end of World War II.

The federal government has begun to deal with essentially local problems—such as sewage disposal, air contamination, and water pollution—because it has the money. This is the fact of life that we face today in searching for solutions to these and other environmental problems. The only source of funds that cannot be diverted from priorities such as welfare and basic education is the federal government's income tax revenues. Until we wind down the Vietnam War, until we diminish defense expenditures, until we assign new priorities to the federal income tax dollar, money with which to attack our environmental problems will not be available at the local or state level, except in our wealthiest communities.

Another aspect we should recognize is that local government—based as it is on the property tax and guided as it is by a national tradition of promoting development, commercial enterprise, success, and growth—is nearly everywhere in the United States under the control of developers. That means either the Chamber of Commerce or men who want new industry and commerce to come into their area to increase the property-tax base for better schools and civic services, or to bring in fatter payrolls that would make their neighborhood more prosperous.

Look at the remaining open space of this country; for the most part it exists in the rural counties.

Let me cite the example of Lake Tahoe, which extends into two California counties. At South Lake Tahoe lies Eldorado County, traditionally one of the poorer California counties, unable to provide proper education, welfare, and services. World War II was followed by the construction of a major highway to South Lake Tahoe, the development of gambling on the Nevada side of the state border, and a sudden influx of people seeking gambling or outdoor recreation. South Lake Tahoe became a new bonanza for the County of Eldorado.

But there is no likelihood that Eldorado County will be able to control water pollution, air pollution, or the diminution of open space. Local government cannot handle the problems of environmental pollution because it is still dedicated—and *must* be dedicated under its tax structure—to development and promotion of growth.

What is the answer?

I have two rather novel suggestions. Essentially they are based on recognition of the fact that the sudden change in demand from development to conservation requires us to deal rapidly and effectively with our institutions and laws, and to turn them toward the same priorities that we insist on but find ourselves helpless to achieve at the local, county, and state levels. There must be recognition that the problem is a federal one and that federal standards are necessary to eradicate pollution.

A man who builds a pulp mill in Maine and pollutes the Penobscot River can deal with local government; he can say, "If you increase your pollution control standards, I will have to move my plant to South Carolina." A company that pollutes the Shenandoah River in Virginia can say to the state or local government there, "You cannot insist that I stop polluting the Shenandoah River; if you do, I will close my plant and move where the standards are less strict."

Clearly, environmental standards for air and water pollution must be national in scope, not subject to the desire for growth, payroll, or property-tax base in a local region where one area competes with another.

In this connection we should recognize that the true enemy of our environment is local government, within which exist pressures and powers that cannot cope with environmental problems, much less regulate them. It cannot care in many respects because quite often the pollution occurring within the geographical boundaries of one government is not borne by its citizens but passes to another regional entity. In California the air pollution emitted from San Mateo County and its highways is blown by the prevailing winds to Alameda County, on the east side of San Francisco Bay. This phenomenon holds true throughout the country, where any single state with lower standards can pollute the waters or air of its neighbors.

It is therefore essential that the first principle in our environmental rehabilitation requires *federal* standards, not just because the only source of sufficient funds to cure the problem is the United States government, but also because local standards will not be equal to the task.

One other ingredient, sometimes not recognized, should be added. In the past decade the federal government has often agreed to make available additional monies for education, sewage control, or other worthy projects if a local government would first pledge matching funds. That policy has come to a grinding halt; it is having a major and adverse social effect because it has often turned out that the school districts capable of providing matching funds for federal education assistance were in the wealthier localities and that the wealthier cities can afford to build sewage plants. The poorer cities cannot pay equivalent matching funds because higher property taxes in their communities would push from their homes the older residents, retired people, and lower-income citizens.

In such areas of continuing population growth as California the raising of local monies by floating of bonds has become almost impossible. The people refuse to vote funds to be matched by the federal government; they cannot afford such outlays in the poorer areas, because the financial drain would exhaust their ability to pay their rent or mortgages, and they would lose their homes.

My two controversial and specific suggestions may provide the necessary ingredients to change this picture.

First, I think we may have to create a federal commission— perhaps even a cabinet office—on waste disposal and pollution. We are beginning to recognize that the cost of disposal of waste air and water and garbage is more than the local government can afford. The source of that pollution is known; it can be taxed for the cost of its disposal.

Let me mention several examples. We know that after some years every automobile off the Detroit assembly lines will pass into the hands of an individual who remains its owner for a limited time. We have seen automobile after automobile engaged in accidents or with engine breakdowns for which the repair costs are greater than its value to its owner. Such vehicles are abandoned on the city streets or in the countryside. Scarcely a streambed exists in many rural areas where some rotting car has not been stripped, pushed over the bank, and left to rust as a relic of our industrial power.

I suggest that the remedy for such blights is to give this national commission on pollution the power and obligation to assign a dollar value to the disposal process of each American industrial product.

If New York City pays a contractor $25 to pick up the hulk of an automobile, haul it to a central dump, and crunch it into relatively small waste, that cost, which is burdening the tax roll of New York and many other cities, might properly be placed on the automobile industry as a $25 tax added to the price of its product. That money should go into a central fund administered by this national cabinet office or commission, which I shall call the Federal Commission on Waste Disposal and Pollution; it then would be used by the commission to create and operate perhaps six or seven central crunching factories. If we must establish such plants around the country and set up regional waste-disposal plants, they should be financed—not by local property tax dollars, but by a federal tax on the product itself.

If we know that there is not a stream in this country any longer where you can cast a trout fly or canoe or enjoy its natural beauty without a beer can winking up from the depths, we could add a four-cent tax on the production of each beer can (if prac-tice, procedure, and the economic state of affairs showed us that we had to pay Boy Scouts two cents to stimulate them to pick up each can and take it to a central dump). At its inception and source no product that represents an eventual waste need be im-mune from our control by this sort of a tax.

I have been fascinated in Congress by testimony of the deter-gent industry's three major producers, Colgate-Palmolive, Lever Brothers, and Procter and Gamble, who turn out something like 500 million pounds of detergents each year. About 50 percent of those detergents are phosphates, one of the major causes of eutro-phication. If the testimony is correct, the 10 million people living in the Lake Erie basin pay about $1 per capita annually for the phosphates that go into those detergents to prevent tattletale gray. Our modern standard of cleanliness requires a cleaning level that to date has been obtained only by the phosphates.

We in Congress asked the detergent industry how to handle the problem that developed after those phosphates had transformed about one-third of Lake Erie into a dead lake by the algal growth they stimulate. The industry responded, in effect, with the suggestion that we should build tertiary sewage-treatment plants so that the phosphates could be taken out of the waste water *before* it flows into Lake Erie. Later an expert witness testified that to increase all local sewage plants in the Lake Erie basin to tertiary quality would require a capital expenditure of about $2.30 per year for each of those 10 million citizens. This would mean that, if we were to follow the industry's concept for disposal of the phosphates and reversal of the eutrophication process (if indeed we can), we should levy an individual, annual

$2.30 tax on those people in the city areas funneling sewage into Lake Erie.

What about an alternative, charging the detergent industry $2.30 for each dollar's worth of phosphate it produces yearly? The addition of that cost at the source might possibly be a better means of paying for the cost of disposal of that particular waste.

Our congressional inquiry disclosed that if such an annual cost should be imposed, the industry then might turn to a substitute for phosphate called NTA, which has been tested for some time and which does not have an eutrophication effect. That would increase the cost of phosphates perhaps 30 percent, from $1 to $1.30 per year, far less than the additional $2.30 per capita tax that would be required for tertiary sewage plant construction.

This is the kind of problem that challenges us in nearly every industry. The automobile manufacturers could devise smog-control devices. A recent antitrust suit was based on a 1952 agreement among the three major auto manufacturers not to promote smog-control devices because they would increase production costs and thus possibly cut sales volume. Almost every industry faces the dilemma that if it applies its technological research to make its product nonpolluting or easier to control in the pollution process, it runs against the profit motive—the traditional fountainhead of American business.

Of course much of the business world has as great a desire to restore and preserve our environment as does the student or conservationist. A growing number of executives in every industry, including some of our worst polluters, are insisting on changes in their operation to recover the environment of their youth, which they now see being destroyed. But we must create additional incentives and mechanisms through the federal government, because there is no way that industry will fully police itself until threatened or encouraged by official action.

For this reason I suggest the concept of a commission with the power to assign a cost to each product at its inception. I would allocate some percentage of such revenue to support research in the field of the product's disposal or ultimate pollution. Although the expertise exists in industry to seek answers to environmental problems, that research sometimes conflicts with the competitive position of companies or may wipe out the profit on which a company survives.

What real benefit would there be to a company making millions of dollars each year producing pills for the birth control market if it should happen across a discovery that, in effect, would wipe out its market?

What incentive is there for the automobile industry to come up with research that would end pollution but might destroy its profit-making capacity?

No jet engine or aircraft company attempted to put a muffler on planes—something that we insist on as a matter of course with automobiles—until several years ago, when two contracts were given to Boeing and Douglas to explore if jet noise could be reduced. The result: the possibility for reducing the noise created by the engines on landing to half the usual noise level; these applied to the Boeing 707 and the DC-8, which are the primary contributors to intolerable jet noise, if they were retrofitted at a cost of up to $1 million per airplane.

That kind of fact is not going to be learned by private research and communicated to the government. The only answer is continuing federal research in these fields, funded as I have suggested.

My second concept relates to the preservation of open space in the United States.

As I mentioned earlier, no local government is averse to extending its boundaries and its development into the adjacent countryside, because by such means it achieves the prosperity and tax base that it desires. Local government cannot zone land to protect open space, because generally such land is taxed on its fair market value as if it were developed or suitable for development—as it usually is. Consequently many farmers are permitting their land to be developed prematurely, because they cannot make a living and simultaneously pay taxes on property directly adjacent to cities. Our present structure of government therefore has a built-in process whereby existing cities grow and grow and grow, until the man who went out to live in the country where he could enjoy clean air and open space finds himself again embraced by an urban environment. We have built expressways around our cities to bypass them, but we have discovered that they spawn an entirely new level of development, until they end up in the heart of new cities.

How then are we to achieve preservation of open space?

Back in 1898 an Englishman, Ebenezer Howard, proposed that belts of land should be set aside in every city for parks and for purely agricultural or natural pursuits. Because of today's tax structure, however, no city can any longer afford to have belts of agricultural land between or adjacent to its subdivisions. No individual can afford to live on such property. We have made tentative steps through local laws. California has a statute, the Williamson Act, to reduce taxes on land maintained for agricultural purposes. But the pressures have generally been too great. When development looms and profit becomes a possibility, the landowner sells out, and more open space is lost.

I suggest that it is now time to consider a national land-use policy and a national land-use commission that would establish specific areas within this country for agriculture, conservation, and urban development.

In doing this we must bear in mind that, under the Fifth Amendment to our Constitution, the landowner has the right to just compensation if his property is damaged or diminished in value through governmental action. This is a historic, traditional, and proper right in this nation.

For example, if we want to take land adjacent to New Haven to preserve as countryside, we say to the landowner (the following values are hypothetical) that his land is worth $10,000 an acre for subdivision development but that we are going to keep it agricultural; thus, his land will have a value of only $1,000 an acre. If that man owns 100 acres, we are reducing the value of his property by $900,000, and he is entitled to compensation.

How can we pay him? Obviously we cannot pass bond issues to acquire open space; there is not enough money in the U.S. Treasury to purchase all the land that we need. But the federal government has immense other powers, and I suggest another possibility.

Every time a federal highway is constructed, a bridge is erected, a road is built to a formerly inaccessible lake, a federal improvement is made, a military base is established in the wilderness, the adjacent lands increase in value. The English have developed a concept that when increment in land value occurs by reason of governmental action, a portion of that increment (I believe it is 40 percent) is assigned as a lien against the involved property for compensating the man whose land is labeled conservation.

We speculate that the United States will increase in population from 200 million to 300 million within the next thirty years. The Department of Housing and Urban Development (HUD) recommended to Congress in 1969 that we develop ten new cities of a million population each and 100 new cities of 100,000; that we keep from piling more and more people into existing cities; that we consider taking areas with available water and the capability of supporting population growth; and that we build new towns out in the country and hopefully preserve the open space between them and other communities. If the government is going to create such improvements and increase the value of some private property, it would seem fitting to assess against that increase some sum of money to reimburse the man whose lands have been permanently set aside for open space.

I would propose that such a national land-use commission be empowered to designate areas imperiled by intense growth and to establish national zoning policy that such land shall be used for conservation or agriculture and not be subject to further development. That commission also should determine where the new cities shall be located and where the increment in values should be used. That increment need not be assessed in dollars against a farmer who suddenly finds that he is going to be adjacent to an accelerator in Illinois and that his land is soaring from $1,000 an acre in value to $10,000. It would be sufficient if an urban land bank assessed the 40 percent lien against that $9,000 per acre increase but required payment only when the farmer developed his property or sold it for the increased value; then the lien money should be paid into the urban land bank for use in compensating property owners

whose lands have been set aside permanently for agriculture
or conservation.

Let me give an example. My county in California is one of the
few regions in this nation where artichokes can be grown. The
combination of seacoast, depth of the soil, nature of the environment, and fogs that hang over the shoreline provide the proper
growing conditions for artichokes, one of the real culinary deli-
cacies. If we do not take these artichoke lands out of the path of
California's rapidly growing population, under existing laws they
will be wiped out completely by residential development.

The same fate threatens the Napa Valley, which produces some
of the finest red wines in the world, and the Livermore Valley,
with its excellent white wines. The peculiar combination of soil,
climate, and environment makes these treasured areas. Local governments in the Napa Valley have tried to halt encroaching development by imposing twenty-acre zoning, an action that may not
stand up in the courts. Under my proposal, that national land-use
commission would have the power to keep the Napa Valley agricultural; if that decision reduced the value of property there by
$5,000 an acre, in due course it would be paid back out of the
revolving fund.

Bear in mind that my proposals recognize an underlying principle: land today is perhaps as important as water and air to us all.
When we talk about taking the profit out of land development,
we are intruding and interfering with a treasured right of the
American free-enterprise system. But what if we do not take the
profit in land from the private developers? What if we do not
materially change the present legal and tax structures that force
this development upon us against the will of the majority?

We dare not lose sight of the fact that the land itself has a
common benefit to us. We must reassert our right to walk across,
look across, range across open spaces. Privately held lands have a
value to us that their temporary owners can destroy forever.

The land has a peculiar capability for production of food and
for recreational enjoyment. It should be considered subject to the
same type of common trust that we have assigned to air and
water.

Social-Sector Industries:
The Challenge of Our Conscience

David Carley

It is eight years since *Silent Spring.* The American nation is caught up in crises of pollution and absolution. Rachel Carson's forensic on the indiscriminate use of pesticides was criticized by the chemical industry (yet Monsanto, which launched a particularly vicious attack, now is a convert of sorts and takes full-page advertisements heralding its concerns with air and water pollution). Miss Carson was calumniated by many in the federal bureaucracy (said one member of the Federal Pest Control Review Board, "What's she so worried about genetics for? I thought she was a spinster").

But *Silent Spring,* we now know, did effectively put on trial those who would leap before they look, confiscating—with nothing in mind but immediate gain—the natural world that is all mankind's real capital. Unquestionably, bureaucrats were prodded into action against polluters of air and water much earlier than would otherwise have been the case. The book did for the environment what Michael Harrington's *The Other America* has accomplished in the social sector: a new day in court for the litigation of the American soul. It did for the twenty-first century what Ralph Nader's *Unsafe at Any Speed* has inspired for the world of industry: a long-overdue Nuremberg judgment of Detroit.

Now we are getting at least the beginnings of an inversion, in which the end result of production is viewed for its people impact first, its profit impact second. This is a significant change in our

David Carley is the president of Public Facilities Associates, Inc., a Wisconsin firm that specializes in bringing government and private enterprise together to "package" housing and urban renewal projects. He is also on the board of Scholz Homes, Inc., of Toledo, Ohio. He holds a Ph.D. degree in political science, is former director of the Wisconsin Division of Industrial Development and of the Wisconsin Department of Resource Development, and was executive assistant to Governor Gaylord Nelson (now a U.S. senator).

thinking, and it will continue to affect our nation for decades to come.

It is interesting to reflect that perhaps in the years ahead great careers and even fortunes will accrue to those who devote their efforts to societal—*not* production—problems. Air and water and noise and landscape pollution control; housing; recreation; education; transportation; public facilities requirements—these and other social needs present a market measured in the trillions of dollars and human survival.

On the side of mankind we have about us some astute and able muckrakers and, increasingly, in the political arena concerned men who know that the time is *now*—not because Election Day is always near, but because mankind's time is perilously short.

Superior political leadership should be the objective for the social-sector industries. It is not the total answer or the panacea. But the private sector *must* cease to look away from political leadership; it *must* now give its support to what it once erroneously regarded as inimical to its interests. The corporations of the United States are going to find out that politicians and government officials who espouse the expenditure of funds to protect our environment are, indeed, their friends and not their enemies. For our real wealth is the land, the natural resources, the people. A diminished environment must ultimately cause economic disruption; that is as certain as the certainty of change.

I come from Wisconsin, in which huge paper mills dominate the economy of many regions. These mills are among the state's largest generators of income and the greatest water polluters. This is typical of the conflict we have tolerated between industrial development and environmental deterioration.

Recently I visited Puerto Rico. Copper-strip mining is at hand there. Its backers are telling everyone that industry will bring in something like 800 jobs and that the generation of money income each year will exceed $15 million for fifteen or twenty years. However, many are now concerned that 800 new jobs and the infusion of more money may not be worth anywhere near the ultimate loss caused by the strip mining and what it would mean environmentally to 8,000 acres of land.

Our physical environment is indivisible; houses, dams, parks, roads, schools, and factories are all parts of the same organic system. The sooner corporations, the private sector, and the politicians realize this fact, the farther along the road we will move toward the protection of this environment. We need a creative partnership between the public agencies and private enterprise. We need overall aims and guidance in terms of environment. We need housing goals, too.

Politicians can talk vainly and drearily about our national need for 26 million housing units in the next ten years. I am trying to warn some of my politician friends that we can no longer give this nation's polarized minorities, the ethnic minorities, the poor, and the aged those trite statements of how many housing units we need and then take no action!

Minorities in this nation are finding sophisticated ways to implement their strategies and tactics to force actual delivery of housing. If the private sector, together with political leaders, does not produce the housing we need, these polarized groups will no longer accept the "normal" political process. They will demand, not evolutionary change, but revolutionary change. I do not think the private sector or most of our political leadership realizes just how dire are the circumstances in terms of that possibility.

I am convinced that we will have a relatively tight money situation for a full decade. Perhaps it will not be quite as tight as it is now, but a tight money condition will be compounded, I am convinced, by an increasing reluctance by taxpayers to pay more taxes for critical public-sector needs.

The 1966 Joint Economic Report of Congress, perhaps the most definitive study of public-facility requirements in the United States, predicts that state and local public-facility needs, community needs, energy, gas-distribution systems, and schools (it does not even include housing) will take a capital outlay for the ten years from 1965 to 1975 in excess of $499 billion. We have approximately that amount in terms of our existing capital plant. State and local government facilities come to about $450 to $500 billion. Thus we need a 100 percent increase!

The gap between the public-facility needs of this country and that which is going to be financeable through our ordinary lines of credit is enormous. At least 50 percent is beyond the current funding capability of present systems of revenue sharing and taxation at the state and local levels—even if federal aids are included.

A political backlash is evident in the United States. It is particularly representative and reflected in my home state's legislature, which cut $57 million out of the budget of the University of Wisconsin and also slashed something like $45 million from our state public-welfare budget last year. The people of Wisconsin are reacting; their legislature is responding to them; and they are not going to put up the cash. The same reaction is visible all across the Unites States.

Where will the money come from? The response, I believe, must come from the private sector. This country is moving toward an entirely different kind of public financing, where a greater part of the cash, the money, or the line of credit—or the financial clout, if you please—will be in the hands of the private corporations. The unwillingness of the public to turn over additional revenues will force such a development. If that sector has the money or the line of credit available, enormous power will then flow away from government to it.

For fifteen years I was on the public side; I could not understand why private groups, private industry, would not meet the challenge. Why didn't *they* build the housing? Why didn't *they* build the schools? Why didn't *they* build the capital facilities? What was going on? The market for all of them was obvious to me and to many.

They talked about all the red tape and problems in housing and the "payoffs" to politicians (red tape and payoffs do exist). But the fact is that, by and large, their excuses amounted to a ploy or a bit of camouflage. Private industry preferred to remain in the lucrative consumer market—a market that has had little to do with social responsibility, and involvement with the public market that was relatively untouched by public policy, debate, or regulation. This choice was a mistake. First of all, the *need* was there; second, the opportunities were prodigious.

The concern all of us should have is for the kind of measurement, the kind of evaluation that will be made by the public sector with regard to this incursion into its domain by private groups. No longer can private corporations that use public needs as a market for their goods and services be motivated solely by profit and return on invested capital. Social capital returns are equally, if not more, important. It is imperative that private corporations now find different evaluations and measurements of success for the public or social-sector markets.

The tie between what I am discussing and the environmental crisis is evident. The academic, intellectual, and political concern with this issue has increased during the last decade, particularly in the last three years. Yet the private sector is lamentably far behind the academic and intellectual communities in recognizing the problems of environmental protection in spite of the enormous market potential implicit in those problems. Part of that market potential is the $499 billion in state and local capital-facility needs alone, a total that does not include services or amenities.

One of the most important books published in the United States in the last decade is the *Report of the National Advisory Commission on Civil Disorders,* known as the Kerner Report. Its appendix contains a study of what private enterprise can do in the aftermath of riots such as those that occurred in Newark, Detroit, and Watts. I read with dismay the statements by some of the most important leaders in the country's private sector about private involvement in public problems: the same weary cliches and pathetic anachronisms, all to the effect that innovative creativity essential to the satisfaction of human needs is basically found in the private sector. But the record does not show any great performance there. As a matter of fact, the greatest initiative and concern and innovation and creativity with regard to the satisfaction of human needs and wants—at least in the last generation—have been found, not in the private, but in the public sector.

Then what do we do about providing housing in the United States? About environmental concerns? What does the private sector do about providing for mass-transportation needs? What do we do about answering recreational needs for all of our people, not just the privileged few? What do we do about responding to education and health needs?

One of the leading officers of the American Medical Association said recently that this country, more than any other nation in the world, is overmedicated. The truth of the matter is that Puerto Rico stands ahead of us so far as the response to medical needs is concerned. We are far down on the global list in terms of the delivery of health services. How can that be, with our advanced medical technology and the private sector working, as it claims, in the health field? I think it is high time that the private sector provide a much better system for delivery of health services. How can some of these improvements be effected? That is the question we in the private sector must ask ourselves.

Insurance companies comprise the last remaining large unregulated industry; together they control billions of dollars, with no federal restraints at all and only a series of disjointed rules in the fifty states. Except in a few states that do a fairly good job, the insurance industry really leads the regulators, remains aloof on a plateau above the battle—and profitably so.

One way for insurance companies to participate with conscience and social merit in an area such as housing is by dedicating part of their enormous cash portfolios to the mortgaging of low- and moderate-income shelter. Indeed, if they do not help to fund the need for mortgage money, in time they will face either tough federal regulations or tax penalties, or the people who failed to get homes will turn on them in forms of economic boycotts.

The same story holds true, with regard to housing, for the contractors and real-estate groups. If they will not build low-income housing, either Uncle Sam will become the biggest builder—a situation they say they do not want—or they will be so penalized that they will wish they had constructed those needed homes.

Another way for banks and insurance companies to lever their power of the purse into a better quality of life, a better environment, would be for them to begin carefully screening potential mortgage-loan applications. They would try to foresee the social and physical consequences should the loan be approved and the project be constructed. For example, banking and insurance executives might start to ask about the impact of a shopping center on the local highway system or on adjacent housing; they might ask whether bulldozing an area into oblivion for the quick profit of a developer would add to or detract from the character of the community over the long haul; they might ask about the manner in which, and the extent to which, a subdivision may burden a local school system already short of existing classrooms or may burden local waste-disposal facilities at a time when re-lief—through bond issues or increased tax revenues—is not in sight. The point is quite simple: amenities, conscionable con-struction, the viability of municipal services, all relate very much to the success of the environmental fight we now are in as a people and as a nation; they relate very much to the validity and profitability of what we do.

What are some other techniques by which government and the private sector can respond to housing needs? Millions of dollars have been appropriated for urban renewal. The concept should be that, for the good of the larger public interest, no private re-developer could obtain a first-rate, plush job in which he is liable to have little downside risk and an enormous profit, unless he is willing to take a tough job, too. In other words, he must take a Watts project, a ghetto job, susceptible to fire bombing, strikes, or other downside risks. We need rehabilitation in housing as well as rehabilitation in all public facilities in America. Make de-velopers take a tough rehabilitation job for every good new con-struction job they get, for instance.

By the way, in terms of senior citizen housing versus family housing, Lyndon B. Johnson was most pleased in the 1968 polit-ical campaign to announce that he had provided, through his administration, more housing for the elderly than *all* of the other presidents in the history of the United States. His administration did, in fact, build more housing for the elderly, but it was a credit in only a partial sense. Minneapolis, Milwaukee, my home city of Madison, and many other cities of the United States already had taken care of that problem. It has become acceptable in the last decade to provide housing for the elderly, but it has not yet become possible to build housing for low-income families. Because of racial antipathy it has not been propitious or politically smart to construct such housing.

The government ought to say to every community, "You are not going to build just that lovely building for the elderly unless you are willing to tackle low-income family housing as well."

I believe that we *can* have a mixture of private profit making and the public good. But even though I am a member of the private sector, I shall always insist that the controls, the directions, the planning, the statement of goals and objectives be the responsibility of the public and of those who represent the public. In matters of the public markets, even if there is a private profit to be made, it is the responsibility of the private sector to assure that the planning and development are performed or at least approved by public planners and programmers.

There is, of course, a question of how much profit should be made by the private sector when it is engaged in public-sector projects. I am not sure how one evaluates the amount of profit to be made, but the FHA program limits the profit in a public housing project. Because the costs are certified, many builders do not want to do FHA construction. They contend that one of the principal axioms of private enterprise is not having to reveal the methods of achievement. I think there is an obligation to do so. Why can't all public projects be cost-certified? Why can't we have a reasonable limitation on profit? Perhaps we would have a changing of attitudes and a new concept in the United States of what "capital return on investment" means.

I singled out the insurance companies for criticism earlier, and a logical question that might result would be, "Why haven't you acknowledged that two years ago the insurance companies said they would back up to $1 billion of mortgages in the ghettos?" The backing by the insurance companies of $1 billion of moderate and low-income family housing really was not a unilateral risk on their part; it was FHA guaranteed. I ask that the insurance industry step out and back $1 billion worth of housing that is *not* FHA guaranteed. It can afford to do that.

Do you know why there is not more building of housing in the ghetto? One of the reasons is that there is little or no insurance. The casualty companies will not insure a project in the middle of the ghetto. Their rule of thumb is to refuse insurance within a given number of blocks of the ghetto's center, and somehow the perimeter of the ghetto area increases every time they look at it.

There must be a reconciliation—maybe a forced one—among the huge industries that want to work in the public-sector markets and make profits there. There must be cost certification, I believe. There must be an evaluation first and a reasonable limitation on profits.

I am concerned also about what kind of talent goes into the social-sector business. I do not want to see confidence men in the environmental business. We must be careful about our allocation of resources, not only of money, but also of the talent recruited to work in the public markets.

A possible solution might be a measurement, an evaluation: perhaps a year after the signing of a contract the government could go back and critically evaluate performance before approving its continuation. Perhaps the government should let the private sector work for it on a contractual service basis, with payment determined by the effective achievements at the end of a year. Only those people who really mean business and care about the human condition might then enter the field of environmental protection.

I am not very sanguine about private industry's willingness to undertake costly environmental programs or to respond to our need for housing, schools, waste disposal, water and air pollution control and resources protection. I do not find it a very bright prospect that industry will pick a tough environmental or social project like those I have mentioned instead of a luxury apartment condominium, for instance.

Therefore I say that the government should supply some mechanism to help them with the choice, offer some tradeoffs, where they obtain profitable projects along with the difficult projects. The private sector has made us intensively developed; the public sector has kept us felicitously untouched, with one-third of the nation still in federal hands. Now we must develop felicitously and protect the environment intensively. This is the challenge!

It will require totally new attitudes, concepts, and partnerships—some of which I have described here—if our governments, our people, and our industries are to restore, guard, and nourish this continent. It will require the very best *in* men and the very best *of* men. This is the challenge of our conscience.

Energy: Economics of the Environment

Charles F. Luce

The environmental problems surrounding electric energy are not just the problems of the electric industry; they are society's problems. They are not peculiar to a form of ownership of electric utilities. After directing the fortunes of a large public-power operation, the Bonneville Power Administration, and then serving as chief executive officer of Consolidated Edison, which is the biggest of the investor-owned companies, I find that from the standpoint of the impact of our programs on the environment, the question of ownership is irrelevant.

Although the problems that I am going to discuss involve most immediately the investor-owned segment of the business, which supplies about 80 percent of the nation's electric energy, basically they concern society. A mere change in the institutional form by which electric energy is supplied to society will not make the problem go away.

The tremendous growth in demand is an underlying cause of the environmental problems in supplying electric energy. That demand is going up and has been increasing for thirty years at an annual rate of between 6 and 8 percent, which means that roughly every decade the electric loads double.

In turn, this means that each ten-year period not only duplicates the increased generating capacity of the prior decade, but necessitates rebuilding that part of the machinery or lines or transformers that wore out because of the equipment's limited life—usually thirty to thirty-five years. In every decade, so far as

Charles F. Luce is Chairman of the Board and Chief Executive Officer of the Consolidated Edison Company of New York, Inc. He also heads the National Water Commission. He served for two years in Portland, Oregon, as an attorney for the Bonneville Power Administration and in 1961 was appointed Bonneville Power Administrator. He was named by President Johnson in 1966 as Undersecretary of the Interior to serve with Interior Secretary Udall. He is a trustee of several organizations, including the New York Botanical Gardens and Resources for the Future.

construction is concerned, the electric plant of this country more than doubles.

In the case of the Consolidated Edison Company of New York, our electric load growth is not that great. We double our loads once every fifteen years. Our annual rate of growth is somewhere between 4.5 and 5 percent. Nevertheless, that is a very substantial increase. Expressed in terms of new plants that must be built to meet the load growth in New York City, we must construct a 1 million kilowatt plant every other year. And, of course, old plants must be replaced. We currently have seven large power plants in various stages of construction or litigation.

The electric load growth in the United States is caused only in small part by population growth. The population increase during 1963 was about 1.5 percent; in the same year electric load growth was 7 or 8 percent. The United States population rise in 1969 was only about 0.9 percent, a continuation of its dramatic decline during recent years. Electric loads, however, keep right on going up. These figures indicate that the largest part by far of this growth in the demand for electric energy is not linked to a larger population; it is simply related to economic growth, the per capita requirements. Each person is using more electricity—in his home or apartment or on the job in his office or factory.

To meet this tremendous growth, the electric-utility industry can build various kinds of power plants. There are two basic types, each employing the steam cycle (steam goes through and turns a turbine, which spins a generator operating in an electrical field and producing electricity). In one—the most common—the steam is generated by fossil fuel, principally coal, natural gas, or fuel oil. The other basic way of manufacturing steam is by nuclear energy—that is, by nuclear fission, splitting of the atom. We have not yet reached the point where we can generate steam by controlled fusion, the hydrogen-bomb phenomenon; we are still dependent upon nuclear fission so far as commercial nuclear power plants are concerned.

Although we lean chiefly upon those two ways to generate the tremendous growth in electric energy that society requires, other methods are available. Hydroelectricity used to be very important, but now most of the good hydro sites in our country have been developed. Hydroelectricity supplies something like 18 percent of the electric energy in the United States, a rate that is going down with the decline in construction of new dams and the increase of steam plants using fossil fuel or nuclear fission.

Another form of hydroelectric generating plant does not produce additional energy but enables us to store energy at times when we do not need it for use when it is required. It is called a pumped storage project.

All utilities have an uneven load pattern; demands are higher at one time than at another. There are seasonal peaks. New York, for example, has a tremendous peak in the summer because of air conditioning. There are daily peaks, starting at about 11:00 A.M. and ending about 4:30 in the afternoon, when the offices close in Manhattan. At night our loads drop to a little less than half of what they are during that 11:00-to-4:30 period.

With a pumped storage project, when loads are way down at night, instead of the generating capacity standing idle, water can be pumped from a low to a high place and put in a reservoir to be released the next day during peak hours. Pumping power takes about three kilowatt-hours, and two kilowatt-hours are obtained when the water flows back down the hill, because of losses mainly from friction. Nevertheless, pumped storage projects offer a tremendous savings in capital investment. Many utilities have them. The Tennessee Valley Authority (TVA) announced the start of construction of another big one not long ago.

Finally, besides these types of generating plants to provide the electric industry with load growth, there are gas turbines similar to the jet engines for airplanes. In fact, those which we buy are made principally by Pratt & Whitney and General Electric, manufacturers of most of the turbine engines for the world's aircraft. They operate by streams of hot gas going through a turbine; instead of the spinning end of the turbine, there are gears that operate and spin a generator.

So far, gas turbines are used mostly for peaking power. They are quite expensive to operate, because their highly refined fuel costs about two and a half times as much as that used in large fossil-fired steam plants. More and more, however, these gas turbines are being used to meet peaks in capacity.

Consolidated Edison has in operation one nuclear plant, a number of fossil-fired plants, and several gas turbines. We have proposed a pumped storage project at Storm King Mountain on the Hudson River, but we have not built it because we are still involved in litigation.

Not a single form of power generation is free of serious environmental objections or of groups organized to fight it.

The fossil-fired plants are opposed chiefly on the basis of air pollution. Even though we do our best to use low-sulfur fuels and even though we put precipitators on the stacks at considerable expense, some air pollution is connected with combustion: sulfur dioxide, carbon dioxide, nitrous oxides, and particulates or ash.

In addition, fossil plants heat the water. The condenser needs cooling water to operate. Mechanically the way to spin a turbine is to have a lower pressure at its exhaust than at its entrance. This creates a partial vacuum that draws the steam through and spins the turbine. If the pressure were identical on each end, the turbine would not turn. To get that low pressure, we cool the exit or discharge end of the turbine with a condenser that is cooled by water. When the cooling water leaves the condenser the water is about $15°$ F. warmer than when it came in; if we take water out of the Hudson River at $60°$ F., we return it at approximately $75°$ F.

The nuclear plants draw objections because, first of all, critics claim that there are some harmful radioactive discharges in the form of gases. It is said also—and correctly—that the heat discharged from the condenser of a nuclear plant is much greater than for a fossil-fired plant of equal capacity. The present generation of nuclear plants operates at lower steam pressures and temperatures than do fossil-fueled plants. Thus, they are not as efficient thermally, and the heat discharge between fossil and nuclear is about a ratio of two to three (for each two degrees of heat discharge from fossil-fed plants there will be three degrees from a nuclear plant). However, the rise in temperature through the condenser is still about $15°$ F. We simply have to run more water through the condenser for a nuclear plant with a capacity equal to a fossil-fueled plant's.

Fears have been expressed that nuclear power plants will explode. Nuclear power was born under a mushroom cloud, and it has never fully recovered from that genesis. You could not explode today's nuclear plants if you tried all day. The mixture in the fuel just is not explosive though it is nevertheless controlled nuclear reaction. We can say this over and over again, and still a lot of people will insist that they do not want to live near one of these plants because it might blow up.

Our nuclear power plant is refueled about once a year. It is taken out of service for four to six weeks while the fuel elements are changed. We take the spent fuel units out and keep them under water until the radiological discharges that have short half-lives are spent. Then we put them into lead casks and ship them to a reprocessing plant, where still useful material is separated from wastes, which are buried in a designated area a few miles from Buffalo, New York. (AEC officials say the long-range solution of these wastes is completely manageable for generations to come by storing them in old, completely dry salt mines when we really get into the nuclear power age.)

Objections to hydroelectric projects are well known. They center on the dams, which are assailed by conservationists for changing the natural flow of the stream, altering the ecology, and destroying natural beauty.

The same is true with pumped-storage projects, as Consolidated Edison has found out at Storm King Mountain. Even after the company agreed to put the plant under ground, so that very little of it would be visible, objections were raised that the area was wild—not completely wild, but not industrialized—and that if a power plant were allowed, the area would become industrialized. Therefore, said opponents, we must not let a power plant come into the area even if it is out of sight under the ground.

Curiously the gas turbines have not yet run into serious environmental objections. Their pollution is about the same as for the very low-sulfur burning steam plants.

Solutions exist for each of the environmental problems that I have mentioned; some of them I have touched upon. For the fossil-fired steam plants, the workhorse power plants of the nation, we can turn to low-sulfur fuels. In New York we have gone from fuels that have had about 2.5 percent sulfur by weight down to 1 percent sulfur by weight, and now we are proposing 0.37 percent sulfur fuel for the Astoria plant that we hope to enlarge. The change means that much less sulfur dioxide will come out of the stack. We have installed precipitators (dust catchers) on our coal-fired plants. These electrostatic devices can take 99 percent of the emissions out of the air. Development of new chemical processes will, it is hoped, permit the industry to burn high-sulfur fuel and remove nearly all of it in the stack. A good many millions of dollars are being invested toward this end in several pilot plants, and I have no doubt that in five or ten years its achievement will allow the use of higher-sulfur fuels. Then we will be able to take out of the stacks those noxious pollutants that damage our environment.

In regard to water used for cooling, we have ways to protect the ecology. One is to design the discharge apparatus so that water returning into its natural body (in our case the Hudson or East Rivers) is dispersed without allowing the heat to become so concentrated in any area that either plant or animal marine life is damaged.

If that is not possible, another alternative is the construction of cooling towers. They cost money, adding anywhere from 8 to 15 percent to the cost of power production. They are not very good-looking—they are large structures, sometimes 400 feet high, and some are hyperbolic, thin in the middle and spreading out at the top and bottom. They operate by evaporation and therefore, under certain atmospheric conditions, create a form of air pollution. (Get rid of the water pollution, and we create an air pollution problem!) As I understand it, this is not serious except in salt-water areas, where the evaporative mist would be saline; then problems arise with paint on cars and houses, damage to vegetation, and the like. *There* is a serious problem! Fortunately in saline areas such as Consolidated Edison's, cold water is in tremendous supply, so that this problem of excessive heating is not the same as it would be on a smaller body of fresh water.

I think that we are going to have to develop a dry cooling tower, similar in principle to a car radiator, in which the evaporative process is not used. A lot of research is being done in this field. In one of the South African nations a 150,000-kilowatt plant with dry cooling is under construction. So far, nothing that big exists in this country. Estimates of how much such a device will increase the cost of generator power run all the way from 15 percent to 50 percent. Our engineers believe that the "radiators" required to cool a million-kilowatt plant might occupy from thirty to sixty acres.

Sixty acres in Westchester County where we have to build plants! People would not appreciate that, understandably. Nor do we like the necessity of buying that amount of real estate. It would be very expensive. But I think that in my lifetime in the utility business we will find some reasonably good answers for cooling.

For the nuclear plants there is no air-pollution problem other than the escape of some gases that are very low in their radiological level. For example, at our Indian Point No. 1 nuclear plant, which has been operating since 1963, the level of radiation is substantially less than the natural radiation in Denver, Colorado. The higher we go in altitude, the closer we get to the sun; the less of an atmospheric envelope there is for protection, the more natural radiation exists. The standards set for us by the Atomic Energy Commission (AEC) are so severe that we are substantially below the natural radiation levels in many parts of the world where people live at higher altitudes. So I do not think nuclear plants cause serious problems, although not everyone shares my view. Some people regard it as a very serious matter.

The problem of the cooling water for nuclear plants is similar to the problem of cooling water for fossil-fired plants, and I have already covered the possibilities for construction of cooling towers or dispersal techniques for the cooling water.

The gas turbines, which are noisy, can be quieted by baffles. We spent a lot of money to put noise baffles around them. The result is that they are not objectionable to anyone working on them or close to them, and so far as the general public is concerned, they comply with the city codes limiting decibels of sound.

The supply of fossil fuels is limited, how severely we do not know. When I was in college, we were worrying about the time, which we thought would happen during our lives, when this world would run out of oil or at least when oil would become terribly expensive because of our increasing difficulty in extracting it from great depths. We were concerned about shortages of coal and natural gas and the other minerals of finite quantity.

As time has passed and exploration techniques have improved, our reserves have actually grown larger in most of these resources; but obviously there is an end to the supply of coal, natural gas, and oil. Future generations are going to find it more and more difficult to obtain fossil fuels, particularly if the standard of living in the so-called underdeveloped countries is ever to be brought up anywhere close to those of Western Europe and the United States.

Nuclear power offers the best long-range chance of protecting the environment while supplying the electric energy that society needs. Its great advantage is that the supply does not depend on combustion. It does not create carbon dioxide or all the other gases that are byproducts of combustion. Plants are being designed and will be designed so that any escape of radioactive gases will be within limits that are tolerable and not damaging to the environment.

I think that over the next ten to twenty years, at least, the utility industry can supply electric energy to society and keep our world a habitable place. For example, our projections indicate that we can meet the loads we foresee in 1985 in New York City and still have our part of the environment better than it is today.

We have done a lot already. In the last four years we have reduced our part of air pollution in New York City by about 50% (SO_2 and particulates), a record of which we are very proud. The effort cost a lot of money. Our premium fuels cost our consumers more ultimately, because we do not have a printing press to manufacture currency; we have to collect our cost of doing business from our customers. It costs about $15 million a year more for low-sulfur fuel than it did for the high-sulfur fuel that we used to burn. For various precipitators, higher chimneys, conversion from coal to oil, and all the equipment that is required, we spent about $150 million capital plus some additional operating expenses. That is without counting taxes on those improvements, because we do not get a tax rebate for them.

Looking ahead to 1985, we think we can do even better and at the same time supply the more than doubling of loads that will occur between now and then. However, as there is a limit to the amount of fossil fuel, there must be a limit to the ability of the environment, the world, the United States, New York City, to absorb more and more power production plants.

Isn't it time to examine the growth syndrome that we have had in our country? Surely we must reexamine population growth. I just do not see how—in the electric industry or in our economy as a whole—we can go on with the ever-increasing population and keep this earth habitable for future generations into the indefinite future.

As I mentioned in my discussion of why electric loads grow, population-growth control alone is not enough. We must also ask whether economic growth does not have to be slowed down. Economic growth may be an outmoded, even a dangerous, national goal twenty and thirty years from now. Maybe it is already outmoded today.

Obviously our country still thinks that economic growth is desirable. One has only to listen to the arguments made by political parties for votes to know that no one runs for office on the claim that he has a program to slow down the rate of economic growth. No one expects the Democratic or Republican platforms to pledge that there will be no increase in the Gross National Product, let alone a promise to reduce the GNP.

The whole idea of the intrinsic value of more goods and more services and a higher American standard of living is so deeply ingrained in all of us (I am not excepting myself) and in our culture that we will have to talk about it for quite a while before we take any counteraction. Curiously, it is also ingrained in our great rivals in the Soviet Union, because this part of our society they have imitated, or have done their utmost to imitate, as best they know how.

When Stewart L. Udall and I and others were in the Soviet Union in 1962 to inspect the big power dams, the Russians exhibited some power projects of which they had good reason to be proud. They also showed us a film in which they compared the Soviet rate of growth in electricity with the growth in other countries, including the United States. They did this with a motion picture cartoon featuring toy trains, each with a little flag on it. In about 1975 or 1980 the train bearing the hammer-and-sickle insignia of the Soviet Union went charging ahead of the train with the United States flag. This is what the Russians have been striving for—to grow faster electrically than any other country. They have been imitating us –trying to do us one better.

This growth syndrome, therefore, is not peculiar to the capitalistic nations. It is found perhaps even more in the socialistic world, and of course it exists also in the underdeveloped countries.

The eventual reordering of our national priorities will not come about from Detroit and the automobile industry. It will not come about from Pittsburgh. It will not come about from the power companies. It will not come about from the soap and detergent companies. It will not come about from the food packagers on their own. Of course we should expect greater responsibility from all these producers, and in varying degrees they are responding. But basically they all are going to continue producing what you and I want.

We order our priorities every day. We order them when we decide whether we will ride on the subway or in our automobile. We order them when we decide to buy a Fiat or a Volkswagen or an Oldsmobile or a Buick. We order them when we decide to install air conditioning in our home. We order them when we decide whether we are going to wash our laundry with soap or detergent. We order them when we decide whether we are going to buy beer in noncorroding aluminum cans that are detrimental to the environment. We even order our priorities when we throw waste paper and cans and empty cigarette packages in the street.

While visiting a school recently, I was appalled at the trash and the clutter in its entrance. We talk learnedly about reordering our priorities; and we are worried that Detroit, Pittsburgh, and the power companies are not responding fast enough. But what hope is there for reordering their priorities if we are not just a little bit tidy in our individual lives?

That is the starting point. We have to develop an ethic of the environment—a personal ethic of the environment. We cannot solve these problems simply by pinning them on somebody else or on some big bad institution. We cannot say that it is all *their* fault, and if only *they* would do right everything would be fine, and then we go downtown and buy a six-pack of beer with non-returnable bottles. That simply will not work.

The environment problems are not going to be solved unless each of us takes this matter personally and develops an ethical position of his own concerning the way we expend our economic resources and the kind of market we create for the suppliers of goods and services. If we do this and if we convince our law-makers that we will support them, laws can be enacted that will help to rehabilitate our environment.

Admittedly, a personal ethic of the environment is not enough in itself, but it is the essential starting point.

One problem that seems insoluble by individual decisions in the marketplace is that of agricultural pollution. Assistant Secretary of the Interior Carl Klein recently said that agricultural pollution is more serious than industrial pollution. This involves not just the herbicides and pesticides, but the fertilizers, organic and inorganic, that have raised our per-acre yield dramatically.

When I grew up in Wisconsin, a thirty-five-bushel corn crop had the farmer throwing out his chest and bragging. Everybody looked at him with envy. Now farmers get 80 bushels—and do not brag about it—because they have hybrid corn and along with it a heavy application of fertilizer and other chemicals.

What happens when it rains? Some of the herbicides, pesticides, and fertilizers leach out into the streams, into the rivers, into the seas, certainly with serious impact on the ecology of the streams and estuarine areas, and probably of the oceans. However, if we reorder our priorities to save the streams, lakes, and estuaries, we will inevitably reduce agricultural production. That surely would raise the price of food. At this point conservation would begin to hit pretty close to home. I wonder if we are not going to have to start asking questions about priorities and values even in this area.

The resolution of all these environmental problems is not going to be easy or quick. We cannot answer them with rhetoric or hot air or pious zeal. It will take at least a generation of thinking, talking, and discussing before the issues can be settled and the solutions can be found. But I am optimist enough to believe that mankind will develop and practice an ethic that will keep planet earth a pleasant and healthful place on which our descendants can live.

Action Imperatives for Population Control:
A Woman's View

Stephanie Mills

The decade of the 1970s is the watershed, not just for humanity but even for the ecosystem. It is a decade that confronts us with the choice of life or death, with a choice between Utopia and Apocalypse.

Why are we, the young, the aware, confronted with these choices? Why do we have to be the ones to decide? Why can't we be out wearing raccoon coats and driving around in rumble seats and swallowing goldfish instead of having to exhaust ourselves in the prime years of our life worrying about what seems like an inevitable doom of a planet?

Today we face the population explosion and the environmental crises because of a series of delusions that Western culture has labored under almost since Genesis was written. There is a great line in Genesis: "Be fruitful, and multiply, and replenish the earth, and subdue it." A little later it says, "And the fear of you and the dread of you shall be upon every beast of the earth." How true! The whole thrust of our culture has been to ignore the world as it is—which is to say, a sickly place—and to put a premium on a kind of linear idea of time, whereby we go from point A to infinity in an unswerving path, damning every obstacle we meet—even if it is pure reason.

We believe that the earth was made for us. It is ours to subdue. We think we are, indeed, set apart from our fellow creatures by some sort of magnificent holiness.

Our verbal ability and our memory, which enable us to make

Stephanie Mills is active in the Planned Parenthood League of Alameda and San Francisco Counties (California) as a college coordinator working with students, delivering speeches, and handling liaison duties with other conservation groups. A 1969 graduate of Mills College, she gained national prominence with a valedictory address in which she vowed never to have children because of the population explosion. She later took part in a week-long fast, "Liferaft Earth," which was designed to call attention to the population problem.

tools, most distinguish us from other living things. It is rather interesting that tool making and language are our most obvious characteristics. It is sad, too, that we emphasize the tool-making skills to such an extreme, while we ignore the skills of communication that teach us that we are not alone, that we are not islands, that we *can* relate to our fellowman.

We have been hung up for quite a while on the idea that death is bad. The thrust, particularly of modern science, has been to stop death at all costs and essentially to deny the idea that unless the seed falls to the ground, it will not bring forth fruit. To break the life-death cycle, to continue the line—this kind of desire is typically American. But we are not exclusive in thoughtlessly wanting to move like a plague of locusts from one side of a continent to the other, and then to go either straight up or straight down at a cost of billions, and to ignore our abandoned, befouled nests or the human beings who have been cast out in the struggle.

We have had misguided aspirations. The idea that the earth was made for man has led us to believe that man should conquer the earth. We have measured so many of our greatest achievements by our ability to dominate nature. Obviously it was a good thing to dam the Colorado River and drown the wonders of Glen Canyon. Obviously it was a good thing to build more roads to allow us to take our cars everywhere, or to invent vehicles for us to fly despite the fact that they are rather clumsy relative to the capabilities of birds. All this machinistic consciousness, the ideas of progress and of harnessing Mother Nature, have produced some of the seemingly most significant achievements of our time. It is becoming obvious that the sense of achievement we get from damming a river is about on a par with a child's sense of achievement in playing with his feces.

Such projects are not achievements; they are destructive and fatal hubris. In our drive for infinity we create finiteness. None of us will ever be able to see Glen Canyon. None of us will ever be able to see a flock of passenger pigeons. We may not even be able to know what clean water tastes like if we lead a relatively ordinary life. We create irreversible situations. Things are now lost to us forever. We cannot unbuild a freeway and get back what was there originally. It is an ironic circle.

We get our infiniteness in the sense that we can dominate speed. We can control that. Our lives are just so much more limited, because now we cannot breathe quite as well in our polluted air. There are fewer beauties for us to view because we have become conditioned not to see them when we are traveling aloft at 300 miles an hour. We cannot see much, except perhaps a stewardess, a tasty dish intended to gladden masculine eyes.

In our urge to dominate nature we have developed certain capacities. We have become A-number-one exploiters, not just of the planet, but also of our fellowman. We have become killers, not just of a hundred species, but of our fellowman. Essentially the capacity to kill is perhaps nonexclusive. After spending our history in the decimation of entire species of animals, the jump to genocide may not be so hard to make. After spending our history exploiting and ravaging a planet with total disregard for its sanctity, it is not very much of a leap to the exploitation of our fellowman.

In our thrust, in our striving for infinity, and in our rejection of death, we prize the ability to control death. So, with increasing intensity over the last 150 years, we have controlled death to the point where we have created another natural imbalance that is going to threaten our very existence.

I refer to the population explosion. We disturb the balance between birthrates and deathrates. Death control is not particularly political; birth control is. Someone can tell you that birth control interferes with the natural order of things, but that person by the same token would not refuse a typhoid shot or a smallpox vaccination. Unfortunately the natural solution to the population explosion is to eliminate death control and to allow Mother Nature to take her sometimes hard course.

Our delusions have also led us into an environmental crisis. You may hear almost more than you can stand about both the population crisis and the environmental crisis. They are not quite one and the same, but there is a great degree of interplay.

We are looking the four horsemen of the Apocalypse squarely

in the eyes. Ultimate results of the population explosion are possibly plague—very likely among densely crowded, weak people; famine—a virtual inevitability; war—a result of our inability to communicate, of our exploitation, and of our penchant for killing; and discord—that fourth horseman who often is overlooked in discussions of population control.

I am becoming quite convinced that ever-increasing population leads to insanity.

A behavioral scientist, John B. Calhoun, described an interesting experiment in the *Scientific American* in 1962 (vol. 206(2), p. 139). He confined a colony of rats and gave them all the nest-building material and food they could possibly use. But without birth-control methods they overpopulated rapidly. When they hit a certain ceiling of overpopulation, they began to freak out; they became total social deviants. Mother rats lost all motherly instincts and left their young on the cage floor, where they were cannibalized. Aberrant sexual behavior became the norm. There was a great deal of homosexuality. There was a lot of fighting. Some of the rats simply switched off, withdrew from the colony altogether, and sort of vegetated in corners.

When I read a newspaper I begin to feel like one of Calhoun's rats. In urban societies you see what the concentration of people, the force of sheer numbers, can be in terms of dilution of life and alienation.

The fifth horseman of the Apocalypse is the ecocatastrophe. We are going to have to get him a new horse, put him with the other disasters, and read that as part of the population litany. If I could, I would cite for you all kinds of stupefying statistics, but I would be out of my league doing that.

Impact is of basic importance in the population problem. Numbers per se only begin to mean something when there is a space problem on the face of the earth, when there are literally too many people for us to move our arms. Impact is quite another thing; it is a constellation of four factors: consumption, waste, pollution, and numbers.

America's population explosion is probably severest in terms of consumption, because we are the pigs of the earth. With 6 percent of the earth's population, we consume more than one-third of the earth's raw materials. As a nation, we are basing our strength on a house of cards. To maintain a standard of affluence that is predicated on a shoddy value system which assumes that quantity equals quality, we are exploiting the rest of the planet. We are preventing other inhabitants of this shrinking globe from enjoying even a decent standard of living, so that we may have our Cadillacs, and eat meat 365 days a year, and have antiballistic missiles, and drive from one Howard Johnson Restaurant to another all across the country.

Yes, we are the pigs of the world. We bring in metals, particularly from South America. We bring in food. Possibly the most heinous example of this importation of food resources is our taking of 80 percent of the Peruvian anchovy catch and turning it into meal for our hogs and our chickens. So enjoy your bacon tomorrow morning, Americans, because probably some Peruvians are dying for your privilege.

We consume fantastically; we waste; we negate the life cycle; we have at this point no intention of recycling any of our bounties. We feel that we can act in total ignorance of the operation of the planet. We do not return anything to the earth. We purify our sewage, rather than use it to fertilize our crops. We even purify our crops of their natural predators.

Obviously we threaten our existence with pollution—not just physical, but also mental pollution. We pollute our minds with the idea that it is more important to have endless reams of print-out sheets and punch cards for our computers than it is to have forests. We pollute our minds with the idea that creekbeds are less important than freeways. We pollute our land by achieving these things.

We homogenize our environment. We eliminate diversity, which is a cardinal sin. We make our surroundings more vulnerable through pollution. We create fantastic occurrences; they are much like paintings by the Dutch master, Hieronymus Bosch. We set rivers on fire with our effluence. Recall the burning in 1969 of the Cuyahoga River, which had been declared a fire hazard for a couple of years. The solution there, evidently, was not seen by the officials involved: to clean up the river rather than to patrol it with fireboats, which is what they did. When we turn our waters into a sewage system, when we have caused lakes to die—when we commit such vile acts, we pollute not only our earth but our heads. Possibly the greatest problem that we face is head pollution.

We have our numbers, 200 million of us. The pessimists tell us that there will be 300 million within another thirty years, and all seem to be gravitating toward California and New York. I promise to do you a favor; I won't come to live in the East if you won't come West.

We want to urbanize. We want to go where the action is, so that once we have gotten a piece of that action, we can return to the suburbs and try to regain a little of what we lost by creating a city. When we reach the cities, we find that the intensity of our lives is totally diluted. Most executives today hold one-third of a job. There simply are not that many meaningful careers available to 200 million people. It is almost impossible to get a job saving the world, if that happens to be our fancy. We crowd ourselves in, and we become alienated.

We lose total contact with the forces that shape our lives. I have never seen the man who bakes my bread. I have no idea who built my car. I have no concept of who made my clothes. No one who shapes my existence in a physical sense is near to me. I do not have access to a craftsman because I am not wealthy. All of these social deprivations erode the psychological quality of our lives. We have become totally detached from everybody who produces our goods and also from our government. Our access is so limited at this point that we are lucky if we know who the cop on our beat is.

As we lose touch, we create artificial societies. Maybe we join a professional organization so that we can be further homogenized and talk to a lot of lawyers all the time, or doctors, or Indian chiefs—if any of these happens to be our profession. We lose individualism when we come to college. If we come to a relatively large college, we put our name on an IBM card and attend classes with many people.

Our whole ability to be individuals is limited, because our free-doms are eroded by the pressure of numbers. It is not illogical to yell and scream about law and order in a society of 200 million people. It may be unpardonable, but it is not illogical, because 200 million people have a fantastic potential for chaos. To some extent law and order simply mean bureaucratization. As popula-tion multiplies, all of our vital statistics will be recorded to the end that, through the least personal means possible, society can keep tabs on its members and maintain a semblance of order beneath which rules chaos. Our freedom will then erode and our individualism will be lost; we shall become alienated and our opportunities for intense experience will be limited.

All these calamities are simply factors of too many people. The problem of numbers is not the sole cause of any of these evils, but the factor of intensity is in all of them. I do not think that we will find solutions to any of them without a stabilization of popu-lation growth. The more our numbers grow, the farther away we move from a realistic concept of the quality of life, and the more we must substitute material things for the aspirations of society as a whole.

I have mentioned that we consume the lion's share of the goods on earth. The net effect is to make ever truer the truism that the rich get richer and the poor get poorer because, although the United States population will double in seventy years, the popula-tions of many other countries duplicate much more swiftly.

People in underdeveloped nations are in the position of being told that they can aspire to our way of life, and they want to (we have translated thirst into the desire for Pepsi-Cola). They think that they can attain our stage of well-being and stay there, al-though we alone require more than 30 percent of the earth's goods. At the same time that this delusion is being circulated, their populations double every twenty to thirty years, which means that all of their growth capital is eaten away to maintain the status quo—if they are lucky!

The combination of this falling behind and never-to-be-devel-oped status of the underdeveloped nations and the ever-increasing dependence of the United States on the importation of resources does not lead toward world peace by any means. It condemns this nation in the eyes of the world. It belies any good intentions that we may have. Therefore, to solve the population explosion, the American family must reduce its reproduction to two children first. The two-child family may be equated with peace. It makes no sense for us to arrive in Colombia in a shiny black Cadillac, extend our manicured hands bearing pills, and say, "Heathens, limit your reproduction." That is no way to establish trust or confidence. It is a good way to condemn all our efforts.

Under the heading of differential impact comes the fact that an American baby is fifty times more of a disaster for the environment than is an Indian infant. An affluent middle-class American child is going to prove many times more disastrous for the environment than a poor child. Affluent WASPs (white Anglo-Saxon Protestants) grow up thinking that they need Triumphs or Sprites, an endless wardrobe of clothes, phenomenal amounts of food—including some to throw away—and ultimately perhaps a Cadillac. Poor people may want these things, but they cannot consume them the way we do. So, finally, the burden of beginning to solve the population explosion falls on our shoulders, particularly and obviously on the shoulders of the young, at least those who are young enough to reproduce.

Actually we can contribute very heavily to a solution of the population problem and might even see tangible results. If everybody who realizes the responsibility of having no more than two children would tell ten people about it and ask them—just like a chain letter—to repeat the message to ten others, we might see an actual decline in the birthrate. This aspect of the problem can be very much in our hands. We should put the lie to the idea that it is the welfare mothers, or the blacks, or the greens, or the polka-dotteds, or the one-handed Latvians who have contributed to the population explosion.

Wherever I lecture, a college-educated woman in the back of the room asks, "Shouldn't college-educated women have more children than anybody else because they have had the advantages?" My only reply is that if college-educated women are so well put together, they ought to be able to *adopt* all of their children.

There is a real danger that awareness of the population problem will be projected as blame onto other groups. A distant undertone of racism exists in everybody who seems to recognize the population explosion but blames it on the other guy. If they are aware of a global population explosion, they acknowledge it and say that it is terrible *in India.* If they recognize the American population explosion, they probably favor sterilization of all welfare mothers; but they never say, "Yes, it's me because I am a pig, and I drive two cars, and I throw tons of garbage into the environment, and I read *The New York Times* every Sunday and chop down vast forests on that account."

As you go through your daily routine, ask yourself where it all came from, and not just in terms of whose wallet paid for it. Where did the power come from? Where did the water come from? Where did the paper come from? What was destroyed in the process of getting it, whatever *it* may be?

There is more to the problem, obviously, than mere survival. Conceivably we could pay every price to survive and accommodate billions more people. We could throw geodesic domes over all our cities and create artificial environments. We could ask the government to sterilize everybody who has had two children. We could even, perhaps, practice some genocide. All of these would be "solutions." Perhaps they would guarantee some measure of brute physical survival. But survival for what?

It is not unusual for species to die. It is not unusual for planets to die. Perhaps this is all part of a greater picture, and it is legitimate to ask: is this an inevitability?

It looks like it, but there is a chance you can opt out of it. If you do decide to survive, the quality of life must be defined. Quality of life includes diversity, and freedom, and good environment. The mechanics for survival are available to us in the political arena, but survival techniques can only be implemented on an individual basis.

This is the difficulty. Nothing less than a revolution in human consciousness is required to solve this problem and head for Utopia instead of Armageddon. The government can do many useful things; it can try to limit our reproduction. But it has been pointed out that if there were a national limitation to two children per family, everybody would run away to Mexico and have a third. Judging from our experiences with Prohibition, this expectation is probably right.

If we really want to live, we have got to change our notions. We have got to evolve new value systems. We have got to reject boosterism. We have got to realize that uncontrolled growth is the ideology of the cancer cell. We cannot applaud when our Chambers of Commerce tell us that our population will double in forty years because industry has arrived. Putting a premium on such growth is believing a fairy tale.

There can be no perpetual growth, just as there can be no perpetual motion. Ultimately we are going to run out of all the inputs for our growth, for our present value system. We are going to have to reject our fetish for gadgets. We are going to have to stop equating quantity with quality, more with better. We must abandon these ideas, and in the way we spend our lives from day to day we must change our attitudes toward reproduction.

At this moment in time almost everything in our culture is aimed toward reproduction: the image of the American family as a sanctified thing; the nuclear family of a man and the wife; the concept of the old maid as a bitter, sad, little old woman who never got married somehow; the idea of the lonely bachelor, poor miserable guy (I suspect that view was created by the old maid); the brutal treatment that these unwed people receive at endless dinner parties intended to get them married, to be one of *us;* the kinds of pressures that childless couples are subjected to by prospective grandparents, constantly questioned about their fertility and about the time when knitted booties will be needed.

All these situations sound funny, but they are very real. From the day we begin to read, nobody tells us that there is any way to live other than in matrimony and with children.

This is not to say that marriage is not a central institution or that bachelorism ought to be the norm. I do say that if we are going to survive in a relatively stable population, we must work toward the development of a kind of mosaic society, where many different ways of coping with our sexuality coexist happily. Thus, you men can be bachelors without being condemned. Thus, we women can remain unmarried without humiliation. Thus, we can marry and have no children. All of these possibilities need to be accepted. Obviously this attitude implies a change in the role of women.

My discussion was given advance billing as "a woman's view." I hope that for the most part it is a *human* view. But I think it is probably worthwhile to digress to the subject of women's rights because they are crucial to survival.

It is impossible to get people to curtail their reproduction unless they are offered an alternative satisfaction. You cannot go to a woman who has nothing else to do in her life but raise children and command her to forgo children. Perhaps one solution, then, is to give women at least an equal crack at the jobs men hold down. And we might start to consider the concept of a woman that is not dependent upon her ability to reproduce or to function as a sexual object. I do not think it is absolutely essential to women's rights that we all take karate classes; nor do I believe that much purpose will be served by throwing away our brassières. I do regard taking cases of discrimination in salaries and employment opportunities to court as potentially valuable. I do favor working toward the concept of a totally female woman who does not have to be a mother.

A woman who is more than an object is also a human being. That is important for both men and women to recognize. At present our culture is pervaded by the notion that women are essentially tasty little morsels to look at.

Remember my mention of the stewardesses? That is one way airlines sell tickets: they tell us that they have beautiful creatures walking around in their airplanes who, incidentally, will serve us dinner and perhaps even utter a word if they can generate sufficient resources for such strenuous labor.

Most of my classmates at Mills College, although as mentally competent as men, went out and were pressed into neoslave jobs. They were regarded as a secondary sex, and now they are piloting typewriters. Perhaps some of them even became topless dancers. That is one advantage of the San Francisco Bay area: you can get yourself a nice, well-paying job if you are a college graduate. One bar will employ only college graduates in the liberal arts to dance topless. I guess that says something about liberal arts as well as college. The bars do not specify physicists or biologists.

The involvement of women as individuals in society is necessary, too, because we are enmeshed in so many crises and need all the resources that can possibly be mustered. Psychologist Carl G. Jung, commenting in his works about the feminine principle, noted that one reason for society's utter objectivity and lack of tempering subjectivity is that the masculine principle has been allowed to become the dominant, guiding factor in thought. This is a nebulous area, but I suspect that at the very worst women could not run the world any more poorly than men have done. Hopefully, more women will become involved in politics. I suppose women are like black people, although the situation is not nearly so desperate; they need images of success who are not devoid of their femininity.

In many cases marriage is a copout for women. It is a career. It is a way to make a living. It offers a certain amount of security. (Men, think that over when some sweet young thing accepts your proposal to wed!)

Our whole attitude toward the raising of children will have to become a little looser. Holding them in common, obviously, is one way to be exposed to children (who are always the salvation and always the wisdom) without having to grow your own. Communes are typically regarded as a province of long-hairs, but many suburban mothers contribute unconsciously to communes in which the children of a neighborhood essentially gravitate to the one woman who really wants to be the mother and leaves the rest free.

Evidence abounds that all kinds of rigid institutional concepts are degenerating. Divorce rates are very high. Perhaps one form of marriage is not sufficient. In the 1920s a Colorado judge, Ben Lindsey, advocated companionate marriage, a simple contract that involved pledging *not* to have any children. The bond could be dissolved by mutual consent. Possibly this kind of institution could be offered as one alternative to our current marriage mores. Maybe we should institute American kibbutzes.

Of course our common concept of parenthood needs to be generalized, too. Parenthood is not simply the privilege of pointing at a child and saying, he has Uncle Fred's eyes and Aunt Madge's elbow. Parenthood connotes environment more than heredity; but many people are convinced that, because of their genetic structure, they can transfer intelligence to another being only by procreation. Adoption has been overlooked too frequently, although it really should be strongly supported. The concept of love for children should not be dependent exclusively on flesh and blood, and we should get off the idea that children are possessions.

In too many circles the ability to support four children and to put them all through college has become a status symbol. The idea that we should have as many children as we can afford is not uncommon; certainly it was the norm in the post-World War II era and is still the viewpoint of many people.

All the changes in attitudes that are essential for ensuring mankind's survival are so revolutionary, as San Francisco poet-author Michael McClure has observed, that even the revolutionaries will be caught with their pants down—and they realize it. It is virtually impossible to imagine an American orienting himself totally away from the beliefs and customs of a lifetime, from every material object that he possesses, and moving into harmony with the earth in an appreciation of what is truly real: the healthy ecosystem (if we can restore it), freedom, justice—all those "corny" old ideas. This is *survival.*

Look at what we have going for us toward guaranteeing that revolution:

First, young people of all ages are flexible. Many are experimenting with different ways of life and families and patterns of consumption. Hippies evidently are ecologically sound. Bathing is wasteful as a compulsion; it uses up too much water. We probably should not bathe unless we smell bad. Recycling clothes—as buying them at Goodwill—is sound practice. Vegetarianism is not a bad idea, and farming your own foods makes sense. I suspect that some people in the suburbs may get a little flak for trying to grow corn in their front yards, but it is worth a try.

A second thing that we have going for us, particularly in the United States, is our World War II experience of recycling. It was considered unpatriotic to throw away aluminum foil. All kinds of materials were recycled; consumption of certain goods was cut back by civilians; victory gardens were grown.

My point is that precedents have already been established; they emerged in a crisis situation—which is certainly what we have now. The widespread concern with our environment offers a lot of potential. David Brower of the John Muir Institute quoted Pogo in his paper: "We are faced with insurmountable opportunities." This is very true. Our environmental crisis and the need to find swift solutions does unify us. Once you become actively involved, you discover yourself conversing with people to whom you would not normally dream of talking, and you find out that in their ways they manifest genuine concern for these same ecological problems threatening our survival.

There is no exception to the rule of environmental disaster. There is no way to buy yourself out of it. It leaves no one untouched. Therefore, if this potential for unification could be seized, it would give us a tremendous advantage, because we cannot hope to endure in a divided country. Survival is impossible if we become so alienated that we regard each other as bearing labels—blacks, whites, effete and impudent snobs, or whatever. Once you have labeled others, you cannot hope for cooperation; you cannot work together to save the world.

This fact holds true for nations as well as for individuals. National boundaries make no ecological sense whatsoever. A system of anarchy among nations has no survival value. Global police actions to remain king of the mountain assure no survival value. The whole business of war obviously has only death value. A certain amount of money is required to get our environment back on its feet. That money has to come from somewhere, but it cannot come from essential domestic programs, which are already financially hard-pressed. It must therefore come from the war budget—which takes us back to the necessity for peace.

Finally, I think the current great resurgence of spiritual values will probably save us. The great surge of religious emotion and concern is not a Christian revival, but most of us are experiencing a need for some contact with God. We are comprehending that even the tiniest segment of the ecosystem's operation is a very holy experience. There is something indescribably magnificent about the interaction of living things and the way that this planet functions and the beauty and serenity of nature. This reintroduction of God provides the kind of force that is indispensable in our struggle for survival.

Until recently the environmental picture appeared to be totally black. If you are a literal believer in everything that you hear from the best scientists and population biologists, it *is* totally black. The only exception is one tiny corner of light: the growing public concern about the problems of our natural surroundings and resources. The founder of Ecology Action, Cliff Humphries, said that pessimism has no survival value, and that is true. It is probably impossible to save our world if we feel there is a gun at our head; that might make us very nervous, and we might not follow the wisest course.

But it *is* possible to save a world. It is possible to create Utopia out of chaos by working toward a revolution in thought and in existence. It cannot be done with a glossy, shallow Madison Avenue approach. It must be done with individual contact. It must be done through education. We cannot advertise a revolution in consciousness. We can advertise just about everything else but not this.

Individuals are the key. A phenomenal amount of effort and time and concern must be utilized to reach all the individuals who need to be educated. Ultimately our greatest resource for solving our environmental problems is our own humanity. Not our gadgets. Not our bureaucracies. Certainly not our weapons.

We must pin our faith on our ability to communicate, to convince, and to offer the alternate satisfaction of a truly good existence that is not predicated on electric toothbrushes and having four or five well-clothed and overly fed children who go to the best of schools.

We must quickly make it understood by all of the world that mankind's situation is analogous to being stranded in the wilderness with a rusty old jackknife as our only tool for survival. We may really be furious if that knife is all we own, and it is rusty, and we have had it since we were twelve, and it doesn't work too well. But we cannot just throw it away and sit down and wait for a helicopter to drop twenty pounds of supplies. That helicopter may never come.

We must hit home, through the educational process, that our environment is not a Davy Crockett-hat fad. We cannot just put it on and take it off, because if we take it off, we are going to die. Ecology, if it is a fad, is the last fad.

Is Clean Air Possible in an Industrialized Society?

Richard D. Cadle

Smog and air pollution have been with man ever since he discovered fire and learned how to use it. In spite of this fact—or perhaps because of it—he has learned that air-pollution control is anything but a simple task.

Perhaps the first really serious attempt to control pollution on any wide scale was undertaken in 1273 when a mandate was issued to prohibit the burning of coal in London. Many years later a royal proclamation by Edward I ordained that no factories in England would be permitted to burn coal; at least one violator lost his head as a result of this edict, which proved to be very unpopular and was apparently abandoned. Elizabeth I issued an order to prohibit coal burning during sessions of Parliament.

The first air-pollution ordinance in the United States, apparently established by St. Louis in 1876, required that every factory smokestack must extend at least twenty feet above surrounding buildings. Since nothing was stated about what came out of the stack, it was not a particularly effective law.

Most people in the United States have experienced smog and air pollution to some extent. Smog is not confined solely to our large cities; small cities and towns and freeways may be smog producers. The type of experience can vary markedly, however, because smog itself varies considerably from one area to another and from time to time in the same region. It is useful to differentiate, in the first place, between smog and other types of air pollution. It is rather artificial but valuable to define industrial air pollution as a sort of single-source pollution that may come from

Richard D. Cadle is head of the Atmospheric Chemistry Department at the National Center for Atmospheric Research, Boulder, Colo. Previously he was Chairman of the Atmospheric Chemical Physics Department at Stanford Research Institute. He has focused his research on analyses of atmospheric contaminants, studies of aerosols, and investigation of the kinetics and photochemistry of chemical reactions in the atmosphere. He has written many articles for scientific and technical journals and is the author of three books on fine particles.

one smokestack or from a single plant that has a number of stacks. Of course when this type of pollution is mixed with other pollutants, it may ultimately form part of smog. It is nevertheless useful to differentiate between this and other pollutants, because the concentrations to which plant life and people are subjected may be much higher than those we normally encounter and consistently call smog.

Radioactive fallout is another type of air pollution; it does have the potential to destroy a large part of the earth's population.

The term smog is a combination of the words smoke and fog. It is a type of community-wide pollution that generally has a multitude of sources, all possibly of the same kind, as in the case of the automobile. It is responsible, at least in some places, for eye irritation and in most places for damage to plant life. It practically always decreases visibility, and in general it is very unpleasant to experience.

Different kinds of smog can be distinguished, but most smog that we encounter is one of two kinds—or, in most cities, a combination of them.

The coal-burning type has plagued mankind the longest and prompted the London edict in 1273. It is composed either of smoke or a combination of smoke and fog, with the fog droplets forming on the smoke particles as condensed nuclei. The London fog of December 1952 that killed something like 3,500 people was of this coal-burning type. It is true that these deaths were not recognized until morbidity figures were examined after the fact; it is also true that most of the victims were already suffering from cardiac or respiratory ailments, but I am sure this fact did not make them any happier as they met their unfortunate fate. Most of the before-and-after photographs that were so popular a decade or more ago to show the effectiveness of various smog-control devices depicted this type of atmospheric pollution.

Photochemical smog has plagued many cities in the western United States. Los Angeles is infamous for this type. Its name originates from the fact that most of its unpleasant properties result from products of chemical reactions induced by sunlight. These reactions involve contaminants emitted into the atmosphere, where they are transformed into other products that are largely more unpleasant and more harmful than the originally liberated substances. In a sense, it could be called a cleaner type of smog (if there is such a thing), because the particles are very small, with no tendency to fall out as soot does in smog of the smoke-and-fog variety. Photochemical smog is also more difficult to control.

Smog from coal combustion is decreasing to a considerable extent, at least in the United States. Part of this decline is merely apparent, and part of it is real. We tend to put more emphasis on the apparent part as we become more adept at recognizing photochemical smog. The real part is evidenced by the fact that this country, over the last couple of decades, has been changing from a largely coal-burning to a petroleum-burning economy. The sale of gas-fired home heaters increased from 600,000 in 1950 to 1 million in 1959, while the sale of coal stokers decreased from 20,000 to 12,000.

The fact that coal emits more contaminants than most other fuels is demonstrated by the results of a recent study by the Los Angeles Air Pollution Control District. They showed, for example, that a typical steam-power plant burning coal might emit 1,915 tons of sulfur dioxide and 3,000 tons of particulate matter per day, while the same plant burning natural gas would emit less than one-half ton of sulfur dioxide and less than five one-hundredths ton of particulate matter per day.

If I seem to emphasize photochemical smog, it is for the reason that I have just given, its increasing importance. Another reason: the coal burning type is easier to control, possibly because we have lived with it longer and have learned to control it a little bit better.

Most of the early scientific work to combat photochemical smog was done in Los Angeles, where it seems to be particularly intense. That region has a long history of air pollution. Three centuries ago Spanish explorers reported that the Los Angeles basin seemed to be a territory of fires and smoke; presumably the smoke was produced by Indian campfires. That sort of comment crops up throughout the history of Los

Angeles, and a picture taken about 1922 from a hill above Hollywood shows a very heavy haze—probably smog—throughout the basin area.

Los Angeles residents really started to object to the pollution in their atmosphere about 1943. At first the smog was regarded as similar to the type that had long been encountered and controlled in so many other cities. This interpretation considerably delayed proper action, because attempts were made to control factory effluents that really had very little to do with the kind of pollution encountered there.

The first real information to identify it and explain why it was different resulted from studies of some of its effects. It was noticed fairly early that Los Angeles smog caused intense eye irritation and sometimes crying, a sharp departure from effects of the smoke-and-fog variety. Plant life was stricken with a very unusual bronzing or silvering.

However, another effect really led to the discovery of what this smog was all about: the cracking of rubber tires. This phenomenon was noticed in several western cities in the late 1940s. Teams of chemists from the U.S. Rubber Co. twice visited Los Angeles to attempt to identify the cause of the atmospheric pollution. Each was fairly sure that the mysterious ingredient was ozone, a form of oxygen which occurs in small amounts in air and protects terrestrial plant life from lethal ultraviolet radiation. Laboratory experiments indicated to these chemists that this cracking of rubber tires was caused only by ozone. Their analyses (by A. H. Nellen and his coworkers[1] and by A. W. Bartel and J. W. Temple[2]) showed that not only Los Angeles but many other western communities had very high concentrations of ozone, many times the concentrations normally to be found in the atmosphere nearest ground level.

The second major finding was by Professor Frits W. Went, at that time of the California Institute of Technology. He mixed ozone with various organic substances—specifically the olefins (unsaturated hydrocarbons) in gasoline—at fairly high concentrations and diluted these mixtures with air to concentrations that might be found in the Los Angeles atmosphere. When plants were subjected to these diluted mixtures, the resultant damage was essentially identical to that suffered in that city's smog. This experiment furnished the first indication that unburned gasoline might actually be contributing to photochemical pollution.

In the third step Professor Arie J. Haagen-Smit and his co-workers at the California Institute of Technology learned that a mixture of gasoline vapors and oxides of nitrogen and air, again at concentrations that might occur in smog, produced ozone when subjected to sunlight.[3] And finally, in the early 1950s, a group at Stanford Research Institute demonstrated by field tests that most of the organic vapors in the Los Angeles atmosphere (those types that Haagen-Smit had found contributing to or responsible for smog formation) were emitted by automobiles.[4]

These four sets of information have formed the groundwork for practically all the research done since that time on substances responsible for photochemical smog. Today we know a great deal more about it, but all of our knowledge is based on these findings.

Photochemical smog would be much more prevalent if it were not for the fact that the atmosphere is usually an excellent mechanism for dispersing pollutants. Sometimes this natural dilution process breaks down, however. The situation is again classic in Los Angeles, although it repeats itself throughout the country.

As one goes up in the atmosphere, the temperature generally decreases, but occasionally warm air forms over the colder air beneath to cause an inversion layer. The exchange rate between the layers of warm and colder air is very slow, so that essentially a lid is formed. Many of our communities are located in bowl-shaped terrain, and when such a lid covers them, pollutants can accumulate.

The micrometeorology—the actual flow of winds within a confined area such as a small city or a town—often can be extremely complicated; it may be different within the city and immediately overhead in the clouds. A study of this phenomenon is often helpful in discovering the origin of atmospheric pollutants. Communities must frequently find out whether pollution has come from neighboring cities, whether it is formed in a specific area within their own boundaries, whether locating a plant in one place may be preferable to situating it in another, and so on. Obviously if we could do away with all sorts of pollutants, we would not have such worries.

Those are only a few of the complicated situations we can run into meteorologically. Some air-pollution problems really do constitute a meteorologist's nightmare.

The chemical reactions in photochemical smog seem to be triggered largely by the photochemical decomposition of nitrogen oxides that are in the smog, and these are produced by practically any combustion process. A large part of these nitrogen oxides, along with unburned hydrocarbons, are emitted by automobiles. (They are also discharged by other combustion processes and sources, such as power plants.) The absorption of sunlight by the oxides of nitrogen decomposes the nitrogen dioxide specifically into nitric oxide and atomic oxygen. The atomic oxygen produced in this reaction seems to constitute the main trigger for all the reactions that go on to form smog; the atomic oxygen apparently reacts with the organic vapors in the air to form extremely reactive fragments of organic compounds called free radicals. These undergo a large number of reactions—chain reactions in the sense that they seem to reproduce themselves, so that large numbers of products are formed for every new atom of oxygen.

In simple summary, sunlight plus unburned gasoline vapor plus nitrogen oxides plus air is the pattern leading to production of the compounds that we call photochemical smog.

I want to emphasize that, even in the absence of these reactions, automobiles are bad actors. We would get particles. We would get unpleasant gases emitted directly from automobiles, even if those reactions did not occur. But the unpleasantness of smog is tremendously intensified as a result of the products of those reactions.

Visibility decrease seems to be the most obvious effect of all kinds of smog; it often prompts the loudest objections by the public. Nor can we ignore eye irritation, plant damage, and possibly other acute and chronic effects. Certainly it is an acute effect when 3,500 people are killed, as in the 1952 London fog. In the case of this smoke-and-fog variety of atmospheric pollution, one chronic effect is well known: bronchitis. People living in England, where this type of smog is prevalent, have suffered from bronchitis practically as long as coal has been burned there. We can only guess at other types of possible effects, such as cancer and heart trouble. Some comparative statistical studies have been made of the development of such diseases in cities and nonurban areas; their findings tend to implicate the urban areas. The problem, however, is obvious: we cannot be sure that smog is the only, or even the chief, offender.

The visibility decrease results almost entirely from wide scattering and absorption of light by airborne particles; very little can be blamed on the actual gases that are emitted. The identity of the compounds responsible for eye irritation is still something of a mystery, but probably various aldehydes can claim primary responsibility. The plant damage from this type of smog is probably caused by this same kind of combination, as Professor Went concluded: the products of the reaction of ozone with unburned gasoline vapors.

Other types of damage are produced in addition to the previously mentioned plant silvering that is characteristic of photochemical smog. Sulfur dioxide, especially in smog of the coal-burning type, has caused a tremendous economic loss from plant damage. Ozone alone is very injurious; witness the death of some pine trees in the vicinity of Los Angeles, apparently as a result of ozone damage.

At present the main acute physiological effect of photochemical smog on humans is eye irritation, but this situation may not always be true. It is at least conceivable that, if we build up more photochemical pollution, we could begin to record deaths from it. We still know very little about its chronic effects, although there is some indication that even this type of smog causes lung cancer and other malignancies.

Until very recently carbon monoxide was considered to be quite innocuous in smog at its normal level of about ten parts per 1 million of air; while low, that concentration is much higher than those of most other pollutants. Now scientists—especially medical researchers—are taking a second look at carbon monoxide's acute effects, which are fairly well understood, and at its possible chronic or long-range effects. Are there cumulative effects associated with breathing large amounts of carbon monoxide for long periods of time? So far, nobody knows. It is a good sign that the question is being studied.

Similarly, until very recently lead discharged by automobiles was considered innocuous. There was good reason for the theory that, because lead was emitted in the form of large particles that sloughed off the inside of the exhaust system, it dropped harmlessly to the ground. In the last five or six years it has been found that such is not always the case and that, in fact, lead may be injurious to our health and environment. At the moment there is a great deal of agitation to remove lead from gasoline for this reason. I am opposed to rushing into this effort (if we are) without making certain that whatever we substitute is not worse than the leaded gasoline itself. For example, one suggested type of fuel is very rich in aromatic substances. It and other possible substitutes may have the potential, at least, of producing more potent carcinogens and eye irritants than our present gasoline. Genuine caution is required before we hasten to remove the lead from the gasoline and then substitute something that may be worse.

One other pollution "villain," the jet plane, should be mentioned. In a large metropolitan area, where there is a lot of traffic, probably no more than 1 percent at most of the total pollution comes from jet aircraft. There may be tremendous pollution locally, as anyone knows who has been around an airport. But jet aircraft are a very small factor in the total pollution problem. When one gets up into the high troposphere or into the low stratosphere with supersonic transports, the relative amount of pollution from airplanes may be entirely changed. They then become the predominant polluters and might affect the weather and climate.

Carbon particles in the atmosphere result in sort of an inverse greenhouse effect, cooling rather than heating. This process applies to particles from whatever sources. As we operate more and more aircraft, this situation may become important; but at present, throughout the atmosphere as a whole, most of the particles come from something other than aircraft.

Now let us consider possible remedies for the problems of atmospheric pollution. Numerous methods have been suggested for treating the Los Angeles air after smog has formed; some are wonderfully ingenious. One suggestion involved constructing a series of smokestacks to funnel up the dirty air through the inversion layer and away, either by means of blowers or by an updraft from huge fires at the base of the stacks. In a variation of this scheme, tunnels would be bored through the hills that separate Los Angeles from the Mojave desert, and big fans would be installed to draw the air through from the ocean. These ideas were very seriously proposed, as a matter of fact, by competent engineers before they started making calculations of what was involved. The real impediment to these suggestions—which in principle are sound—is the tremendous amount of air that would have to be moved (something like 100 million tons daily) to clean out the atmosphere around Los Angeles. Estimates of the power requirements necessary for such a project indicate that the effort would take the entire petroleum output of the metropolitan area.

Another idea proposes scrubbing the air somehow, either with water or with reagents borne aloft and emitted by balloons or aircraft. Once more we are thwarted by logistics, the tremendous amount of cleansing material that would have to be carried in order to achieve our aim.

So far no really satisfactory method has been developed to control smog anywhere except at its source. Some techniques do help a bit; for example, a factory can be erected where its atmospheric discharges sweep over only a few people instead of many. To my mind this method does not offer a particularly happy situation. We have estimated that in a city such as Los Angeles we would have to decrease present-day effluents by something like 90 percent to cut down the smog to the point at which only an expert could detect it. Such a venture could be extremely expensive.

In considering some of the ways by which we might achieve our purpose, let me start with our modern automobiles. The average car without any control device on it emits something like 900 parts gasoline vapors per 1 million parts of exhaust. The controls currently being installed on all automobiles are designed to drop this ratio to about 180 parts per 1 million, and it is hoped that by 1975 the decrease will amount to 95 percent of the unburned hydrocarbons with only 5 percent remaining in the exhaust gases. However, as mentioned before, such equipment costs money. The Chrysler Corporation has estimated—and I think it is probably right—that such a control device will cost between $200 and $300 per car. This does not take care of the oxides of nitrogen, although it is hoped that by 1975 these will be at least partially eliminated from automobiles and that the concentrations of carbon monoxide will be considerably decreased. We will have the problem of old cars still in use, but as they disappear from the roads, our air should be in better condition.

At present, it must be emphasized, no system of inspection exists in any state. Until such a system is developed, these control devices will be only partially effective. It is very important that we devise inspection techniques to make sure that control devices are kept in good working condition and are not taken off the cars to maintain high engine performance. This provision is just as important as getting these gadgets on the cars in the first place. And the procedure will be costly, by the way. A satisfactory inspection station now would cost around $5,000, and this is much cheaper than previously estimated. Probably the individual would have to pay $5 for inspection.

What can we expect from other kinds of vehicles: steam cars, turbine-driven cars, electric automobiles?

Steam cars will help; but they are not the complete answer. I am not sure that they will be any better than a conventional automobile equipped with proper control devices. Even if they prove to be superior, they still will produce or emit some pollutants. The same, of course, can be said for turbine engines.

The electric automobiles that people recently have talked about so much appear to be exceedingly impractical—or, at the very best, practical only for extremely limited use. None of these cars at present can travel much farther than forty miles without having its batteries recharged—if it is not driven faster than thirty-five miles an hour. With our present economy and public transportation system, this prospect does not offer much help, and the chance of improvement in the near future appears rather dim. Even if we did have wonderful electric cars with all the capabilities of gasoline-driven cars, problems remain that often are overlooked. We would need many more power plants to charge their batteries. If the power plants were driven by nuclear reaction, they in themselves would have problems with so-called thermal pollution and with the reprocessing of their fuels, which does liberate radioactivity to the air. All these difficulties must be considered.

Public transportation has often been offered as a solution, and it may ultimately prove to be a great help. Two problems, however, exist with regard to it. One is the money necessary to install a truly satisfactory public transportation system. More important, how do we get people to use it after it goes into operation?

An excellent experiment is the rapid-transit system now being built for billions of dollars in the San Francisco Bay area. It will be almost fully automated, and the trains will travel at speeds of up to eighty miles an hour. Its service is intended to place riders close to their downtown destinations. It will be a wonderful test of the extent to which people will accept a really good rapid transit system after its novelty has worn off.

In looking for ways to clean up the atmosphere's pollution, we should note that industry is actually a lot easier to control than the automobile. In the Los Angeles area, it has been estimated, the industrial contaminants have been cleaned up to such an extent that only 10 percent or less of the total smog can be blamed on industry. But even in this area problems remain—for example, sulfur dioxide from power plants, particularly where fuels containing high amounts of sulfur are burned. Various techniques are being developed for scrubbing sulfur dioxide out of smokestacks after the coal or other fuel has been burned, and a number of plants are using such techniques already.

Work has been done without much success by the National Air Pollution Control Administration and other organizations on techniques to take the sulfur out of coal and oil. Emphasis has therefore been placed on removal of sulfur dioxide from the stacks after its formation. It is not a very happy situation, but we seem to be stuck with it. It is more of a problem for power plants than for homes.

The burning of old automobiles is another source of pollution. People do not often pay attention to it, but actually it is gaining in importance as other causes are cleaned up. It really combines two types of pollution, emphasizing that environmental quality control must be considered in its entirety, rather than piecemeal. Old automobiles are becoming more and more of a headache as they clutter up the landscape and form unsightly scrapyards. One of the most economical ways to get rid of them is to burn out everything flammable. The result: a fantastic contribution to pollution, at least locally. Development of methods for reusing the steel in automobiles without having to burn all of the non-reusable material poses quite a problem.

Backyard incineration has been a problem in the past and still troubles many cities. Before it was outlawed in Los Angeles, it contributed an estimated 10 to 20 percent of the total pollution in the city's air. I can certainly believe those figures, having seen time-lapse movies of the early-morning contribution to the air of Los Angeles by tens of thousands of little backyard incinerators in the old days. The visible result of their refuse burning was phenomenal.

Home heating has been a serious source of air pollution in the past, particularly in regions where soft coal was burned in furnaces. The recent experience in London deserves mention along this line. In the last few years, triggered especially by the 1952 smog episode, only low-volatile fuel has been permitted in almost all of England. The effect of this requirement, just on the cleanliness of buildings, is almost unbelievable. Formerly, if a building was cleaned by sand blasting in London or Liverpool, it would return to its dirty, dingy old appearance within a few months. Now buildings in those big cities seem to stay clean indefinitely.

This advancement has been effected at considerable cost to home owners; everyone has to pay for such major improvements. The old fuel cost about twelve shillings per hundred-pound bag, if somebody wanted to buy a bag for his little home grate—and this is the way that most of them heat. Now it costs about eighteen shillings, a marked increase in the expense of home heating. That may not sound like much, but over a year it can make quite a difference to somebody who lives on a fairly small amount of money.

Coal burning is not the problem in the United States that it is in England, because to a greater and greater extent we have been going to oil and gas heating. The automobile is tremendously important in this country; in England coal burning was extremely important. The air-pollution situation in the United States could not be improved nearly to the extent that it has been in England by the same legislation.

So far my discussion on cleaning up the air has centered on the technological approach. There are, of course, many other considerations; one is the political approach. Until very recently the control of air pollution in the United States from political and legal standpoints has involved a hodgepodge of local ordinances. This situation has been improved tremendously by the Federal Air Quality Act of 1967, in which various air quality regions are designated. Each of these regions must enact various ordinances, set up a plan of standards for itself, and map methods of meeting these standards. If it fails to do so, the federal government can step in and control the emissions in that particular region. This Air Quality Act has teeth in it; most previous federal legislation intended to alleviate the pollution problem had none.

We *can* clean up the air in our industrialized society, but only to the extent that we are willing to pay for that purification in terms of convenience and money. Fortunately technology is helping to lessen the inconvenience and to decrease the cost. I believe that the public is becoming increasingly willing to make these sacrifices so essential to its well-being, if not to its very survival.

References

[1] A. H. Nellen, W. B. Dunlop, C. J. Glaser, and R. A. Landes, "The Effect of Atmospheric Ozone on Tires during Storage," *Rubber Age* 66 (1950), 659.

[2] A. W. Bartel and J. W. Temple, "Ozone in Los Angeles and Surrounding Areas," *Ind. & Eng. Chem.* 44 (1952), 857.

[3] A. J. Haagen-Smit, C. E. Bradley, and M. M. Fox, "Ozone Formation in Photochemical Oxidation of Organic Substances," *Ind. & Eng. Chem.* 45 (1953), 2086.

[4] P. L. Magill, D. H. Hutchison, and J. M. Stormes, Proceedings of the Second National Air Pollution Symposium, Stanford Research Institute, ed., Menlo Park, Calif., 1952.

Modest Proposals for More Livable Cities

Paul N. Ylvisaker

A real sophistication has entered our nationwide discussion of urban affairs in the last few years. That sophistication does not come loaded with ready-made answers but with more and more questions. We are substituting strong questions for feeble answers. A philosopher at heart, I live happily with these questions, even though I know that one of the basic needs in life is to translate thought into action.

Here, specifically, is what I am driving at. The subject of livability in our cities has reached the national level of attention. For years it was regarded as pedestrian, the kind of topic that mayors —often caricatured as buffoons—were supposed to symbolize. For the most part it was below the dignity of the Ivy League to talk about municipal problems. The questions simply were not entertained.

Now such individuals as presidential adviser Daniel Patrick Moynihan are symbolic of people who, having achieved Ivy League standards of excellence, have moved into the highest Washington level to tackle these problems. They have been stimulated by the negative expressions of street disturbances, the injustices of this nation that emerged at the local level.

The search is on for a national urban policy. The Canadian government is engaged in such a project right now through one of its ablest cabinet ministers, The Hon. Robert Andras. The Japanese government has been seeking such a policy for ten years, the Kremlin for the last five or six. The British government has

Paul N. Ylvisaker was the first commissioner of the New Jersey Department of Community Affairs from 1967 to 1970. He served at Yale during 1969-70 as Visiting Lecturer of Political Science. For twelve years he was with the Ford Foundation, the last seven as director of public affairs, and he led in instituting the Great Cities School Improvement and Community Development Programs. He has been a member of the President's Task Force on Cities, the Area Development Advisory Board of the Committee for Economic Development, and the U.S. Public Health Service Exchange Mission to the USSR.

been working at it in fits and starts since the 1940s and more urgently in recent time.

Attention to the problems of livable cities is cropping up at the national level. But equally noticeable is a deep doubt that answers will easily emerge to provide guidelines for a national policy. It is simple enough to describe the urban predicament; it is very difficult to prescribe for it.

A compulsion leading to ulcers and nervous breakdowns in some sectors demands that we must construct a national urban policy that is to be implemented essentially by public bureaucracies. Such thinking is obsolescent. It goes back to a New Deal syndrome of liberalism, which demands that for any social problem there should be a piece of legislation and for every piece of legislation there ought to be an enlightened bureaucracy extending down from Washington through the states, if need be, to local units and to the people. That tradition is far too simplistic to contend with the complex systems we are now creating and encountering.

The operation of complex systems and the resolution of complex problems hold our attention these days as we search for a national urban policy. I would like to speak in those terms, playing down the usual expressions—urban, cities, environment, and the rest. All of these merely point us back to our fundamental predicament of living and contending with complexity. Understanding what is complex really begins with our own perception, and that is where I would like to start here.

Livability is an extremely subjective term. One of the less legitimate reasons for nervous breakdowns in this area today is our approach with a simplistic or single set of perspectives and prejudices. In our growing sophistication about urban problems we spent the early 1950s taking on the aestheticians, the planners who were trained largely in architecture of the nineteenth century. We told them, in effect, that they had a peculiar, very precious set of values and that their imposition on the urban environment would only cause trouble. But our criticism of the aestheticians implied that we had other mystical solutions that were bound to be more powerful.

Then we discovered that the political scientist harbored certain preconceptions. He wanted, somehow, structural solutions of these problems. He wanted structures to go back to simplistic versions of feudalism, with its emphasis on exclusive jurisdictions and precise geographical boundaries. He came to grief when it turned out that nobody seemed to want the metropolitan government he had designed so beautifully. As a matter of fact, those who rejected it appeared to be the very ones he thought would ask for it—the blacks, for example. The blacks voted it down in Cleveland and in St. Louis because they recognized another principle: to go for such a simplistic statement would merely put them in a larger pool of voters and dissipate their growing strength. Carl B. Stokes would not be mayor of Cleveland today if the political scientist had won acceptance of metropolitan government in the 1950s.

Then came the economists, with their own kind of mystique. They said, "We have a prescription heavily based on the free market. Most of you are King Canutes, trying to order back the sea. You are failing simply because the forces aligned against you are much more powerful than that." We have beautiful descriptions of the urban condition in this country by economists such as Harvard Business School Professor Raymond Vernon *(Anatomy of a Metropolis* and *Metropolis 1985)* in the late 1950s and early '60s.

Although their contributions were extremely helpful, the economists proved to have certain simplistic ways of thinking, certain blinders on them. For example, the law of external economies, which explains why we situate our industrial plants and other economic activities where our predecessors located, simply because we then can borrow on what they already have invested in. Thus we acquire additional economies: the streets, sidewalks, roads, sewers, and utilities established by our forerunners.

External economies govern our urban locations and our urban settlement patterns far more than some of us probably would like. City building that ignores these economies gets into trouble and often proves prohibitively expensive. The Indians discovered this when they built Chandigarh, the Pakistanis when they built

Islamabad, and the Brazilians when they built Brasilia, only to learn—as everyone else has—how tightly bound we are to the past. Like creatures of the coral reef, we cannot live far from the crust of life that gave us birth and that feeds us even in its death. We hang on closely, and we settle closely, and we snuggle closely to what already exists. But when for too long too many of us have borrowed on the legacies of past investments, we discover how high the incremental costs of close and continuous urban development can be, how public expenditures and pollution accelerate, and how the law of external economies shows its limitations.

We find cities of more than 250,000 population develop a geometric rather than a simple arithmetical progression of costs. It is all right for the economist who works largely for the private sector, because he can avoid that. He can shift those heftier costs onto somebody else. But somebody must pay them.

What has happened? Young people, as representatives of posterity, are beginning to pay the full measure of costs that have piled up as a result of too easy an application of the "law" of external economies. We simply cannot accept that kind of mystique, any more than we can accept the simplistic thinking of other disciplines and perceptions.

What biases do you, as individuals, bring to the concept of livability, to the concept of urban development? Possibly you have written into you the same narrowness that defines most theories of education; they can be described almost universally as autobiographical in that they assume, "I was educated well and everybody else had better be educated the same way."

How many of us come to the city with preconceptions that produce impossible expectations and, therefore, great frustrations? Perhaps most of us. It took me a long time to realize that my image of urban livability reflected the form and values that I had grown up with. That recurring tendency to define the world and its problems in our own image is probably one of our greatest hangups in the development of urban policy.

I am not arguing that all preconceptions are wrong, merely that they have dominated—too often without our knowing it—the consideration of urban policy. We are beginning to break loose, however.

Presidential adviser Daniel P. Moynihan almost disappeared into the bowels of the White House for a year to try to develop that elusive proposition called the national urban policy. When he finally expressed his ideas, they came out almost as truisms, such large generalities that they are almost banal. I wish that some day, instead of offering us his answers, Moynihan would give us his questions. They would start very profoundly: Are you content to live with some of the realities of urban development that do not square with your biases? Or must you superimpose some Platonic ideal derived from your own preconceptions? Is the city—New York or wherever—probably the reality and closer to a healthy environment than we give it credit for because we come to it with preconceptions? These questions characterize the efforts to distill a national urban policy.

Another level of current thinking that exposes our own philosophies is this haunting question: Has our system of life become so complex that we are close to the explosion and/or death of the system itself?

While in Toronto recently, I spoke with Hans Blumenfeld, one of our most perceptive urban analysts. We were pondering the reasons for the disintegration of the Roman empire. Blumenfeld said the empire came apart because its inhabitants felt the weight of its complexities so severely that they had to escape from them. They cut out. They just bought out of the system because they could not endure the burden of those complexities.

Test this by your own reactions or by the actions of those who have been deeply involved in our system. How many, with exhaustion, are beginning to pull away? It is not as though our citizens are uninformed about the problems of our society. Rather, the fact that they *are* fully informed leads them to say "thank you very much" and bow out. The spreading pattern of negative voting now may not be conservatism of the older variety; it may be an emotional weariness and a feeling that not a soul among us has the capacity to live at such a high level of complexity, and that maybe the system runs best with a kind of spontaneous anarchy.

I have watched the respectability with which anarchy has again become a philosophy on campus these days. Respectable? Sometimes not. But there is an anarchistic element now that has a certain rationality. It says that nobody up there can order this damn system. As a matter of fact, I would not trust anybody to try, because I have seen those guys. I have seen them up close on television, and I have seen the best of them during the 1960s in New Jersey and at the nation's capital. They still did not lick the problem of complexity.

Go back to the Greek legend of Sisyphus and to the Old Testament story of Babel. Sisyphus was condemned to roll a huge stone up a hill, and it always thundered back down to give him the unremitting labor of pushing it back up again. Babel's is a tale of developing complexity in which God reputedly said, even to his chosen people, "Sorry, boys. I am not letting you come any closer to heaven with *that* civilization." And it crumbled to a simplistic level in which the division of tongues and of nations occurred so that inhabitants again could contend with life.

I think we all have sensed this ominous truth. Therefore we have suspected that the highest circles of discussion about our cities, our urban areas, our complex system are proceeding with a haunting and somewhat melancholy and possibly pessimistic thought: we may have pushed the system to such levels of complexity that it is greater than our capacity to comprehend it or to master it!

How then shall we deal with our cities? The only chance I see is for each of us to start our considerations of urban policy with questions addressed to ourselves: questions of who we are, what our life styles are and should be, and what we individually aspire to become. In short, for each of us to ensure our own mental health—and that measure of serenity and self-confidence that will enable us to cope with the gnawing and sometimes traumatic uncertainties that characterize group life in a complicated system. This is not an easy prescription, nor an easy process. But this nation has seen the destructive results of facing complexity, as we have this past generation, without the accumulated strength of individual self-confidence. The consequences have been inscribed on our walls in the handwriting of panic and repression that have ensued with ghetto uprisings and student protest.

So start with that, and then move on to other thoughts about the complex system. Here is a modest proposal on the order of Jonathan Swift: We are past the stage of poverty programs or model-cities programs. If anything, these have shown during the last ten years that you cannot get there from here. I will argue their merits, but not here. Thrown out to the future, they were lifelines by which we grasped the shore and found safety perhaps, but they were not dependable for further sailing. They were extemporized devices that got us through a rough period when we had little else available.

Now we are starting to learn that additional bureaucracies, programs, and appropriations do not necessarily produce better cities or solutions to our complex problems. To the contrary, they have let us live with the illusion that we can make it under the present system. Unless we reorder some basic facets of our system, we won't make it to· safety.

New York Mayor John V. Lindsay is faced with an $800 million deficit. It may well be that the only workable alternative for central-city mayors like John Lindsay is to declare bankruptcy, get out of the business. Central cities are not going to make it, not the older kind in the system that we have now. Not with the present property-tax system. Not with a political system that allows suburbanizing society to isolate the central city area and let it stew in its own juice.

The blacks, moving now properly toward political representation and eager to take over the central cities, are going to inherit that impossible situation. Heaven help us; we should not wish on the blacks more injustice than we have already. When they left or got kicked off the plantations, we suggested that they could find some pretty good cheap housing in the central cities; then we saddled them with all the economic deficits of an obsolete area. Now American society is encouraging them to walk the political plank of administering bankrupt municipalities.

Why can't the central city make it? Because it just does not have the resources. It does not have the political alliances. It is caught, and year by year the rest of society—in its suburbanized legislatures and Congress—will permit the stranglehold over that doomed area to grow tighter.

Recommending that we declare our cities bankrupt is just a figurative way to make my point. A mayor actually could declare bankruptcy, but it would be politically unwise. It might be the mayor's last political act, and he is not in business for that. However, it would call dramatically to the nation's attention that we cannot let such crises occur.

Thomas J. Whelan, the mayor of Jersey City, has warned the State of New Jersey that he will shut down his community's schools unless the state provides financial assistance. He said he cannot continue their operation out of his own resources any longer. Until the state accepts its constitutional obligation, he declared, his city will not perform its educational function. I really cannot blame Mayor Whelan. I think I might employ the same tactics to make the rest of the system recognize that we cannot expect central cities to exist solely on their property tax. When as tough a law-and-order man as Mayor Whelan resorts to the kind of extralegal measures he once condemned street protesters for, it just goes to show how desperate a man can become when trying to endure the circumstance of the American central city.

We cannot have a healthy urban economy nor a healthy urban neighborhood without basic economic nutrients. Our cities no longer have essential economic nourishment. Instead of consumer income, the older cities have an accumulation of the nation's dependency.

That welfare crisis we talk about is phony. There is no welfare crisis of major dimension in the United States. Until 1985 the ratio of the dependent population—the number of those who do not work in relation to those who do—will continue to rise; it will peak about 1985, simply because people are living longer. By

1985 that dependency ratio will be less than it was in the 1800s. Most of it is insurable because many senior citizens will have set aside funds for their old age.

Rather than a welfare crisis such as we frequently hear about, there is only a crisis in the location of that dependency load; that burden is now placed on the older cities. Nearly half of that dependent population has no possibility of working itself off the welfare rolls by employment. Much of it is dependent for other reasons than "slobbism," or the failure to find work or to take work when it can be found. The problem will be solved only when the nation shares and takes over the burden of this over-concentrated dependency.

The kind of consumer income and free dollars which again will attract private investment should flow into the city—traditionally, out of bounds of the American economic mainstream. The trouble is that government funds for income maintenance expenditures and capital outlays are far too insignificant. I strongly favor a proposal for which former Secretary of Health, Education and Welfare John W. Gardner is stumping this country: that we no longer ask the city to take care of welfare expenditures on its own, but we flow in aid through government dollars.

Those government dollars can take a different form from that which some of us liberal bureaucrats have been preaching for a long time. They do not have to go through a bureaucratic mechanism. They can be flowed as income-maintenance payments directly into the hands of the consumer. This flow, in Keynesian terms, would increase effective demand and stimulate private investment and entrepreneurial activity. The stirrings of such enterprise are already evident in the field of health care, where Medicare and Medicaid programs have assured a market for a growing number of new corporations, both profit and nonprofit. This increase in demand and private entrepreneurial response reduces the overload on public bureaucracies. I am convinced that under proper standards and regulation this syndrome is a healthy and efficient one.

Once the government underwrites these markets, as it has supported every other booming part of the economy, we might get our urban economy flourishing again. Until that time, however, we cannot expect the city to pull itself out of its economic quagmire.

Let me turn to a second approach to making our cities more livable; this has to do with the service sector. We have been running this nation on the presumption that we have primarily a manufacturing economy. Our preoccupation with manufacturing is understandable; since the Industrial Revolution we have wrought a miracle in the mass production, distribution, and consumption of material goods. But a major part of our urban predicament is that our society has not done equally well in the production and distribution of such critical services as health, day care, education, and law. Unless we provide ready and equal access to a proper mix of such services, we cannot say that we have built livable cities—or suburbs, for that matter.

The nation today demands that those services that have been produced on a constrained basis by monopolistic and medieval traditions now be placed on a mass-production basis. The black was the forerunner. He marched in the 1960s to say, "Look at this lousy health service that I've got in the central ward of Newark or in deep Harlem." The rest of the population is starting to realize that it is dealing with an incomplete Industrial Revolution, to which the black pointed unerringly. That incomplete Industrial Revolution concerns the mass production, distribution, and consumption of critical services.

We are going through a new populism. What people on the streets once demanded of the monopolistic manufacturer they now require from the monopolistic producer of these services. Schools and universities are in trouble because the customer is complaining. Doctors are in trouble because the patient has started to complain. Lawyers have been in trouble, but they are sharper than some of the others and have accommodated better with programs of legal services. Everyone who presides over inadequate services is going to be in trouble.

Nobody who is developing urban policy has gone to the place that really counts: the regulatory devices by which these services are put together and produced. State regulatory agencies—notably

those that license and supposedly monitor the various professions
and producers of services—perpetuate guild monopolistic and
medieval traditions of the service producers controlling such
terms as who will deliver, under what kind of conditions, at what
pay, and with what financial requirements. We must break that
bottleneck.

If I were to advise anybody who wanted to go on the next
protest march, I would say, "Don't go to the old places. Go to
state regulatory agencies instead; if you want to do it peacefully,
just listen to them for a while. Find out where they meet and
whom they number among their members." Merely the silent
presence of watchful outsiders would be a healthy pressure to
apply to these agencies. But knowing the closed-room character
of most of these agencies, I am sure that confrontation tactics
will be necessary to pry open what is the public's business, even if
tradition has been to make it exclusively the business of the
several guilds and professions.

This is where the action will be during the 1970s: perfecting the
Industrial Revolution and the democratic delivery of critical
services.

Another facet of our complex way of life is our revenue system.
We will not have livable cities and viable urban economies until
we break loose from the federal monopoly on the income tax.
That is putting it pretty strongly. But the "Feds" adopted the
income tax some time ago and discovered what a high-yield device it is. With a growing economy they have been able, since
World War II, continuously to lower the standard income-tax rate
while increasing their total receipts. And since the "Feds" during
that period successfully avoided getting substantially involved in
paying for this country's plumbing and housekeeping costs, they
had revenue to spare to indulge in disastrous foreign adventures
such as Vietnam.

In retrospect I wish that we had hooked the federal government
into the rising cost of urban government; it would not have been
able to look twice at sending more than the first 1,000 troops to
Vietnam.

Lately, federal authorities have begun talking about sharing national revenues with state and local governments. I happen to think there is a large element of gamesmanship in these proposals. First, the intricate formulas necessary for such arrangements are an invitation to never-ending debate in Congress. Second, even if a formula could be agreed upon, the amounts are not likely to be substantial enough, especially for our impacted urban areas, which are scheduled under the administration proposal to get less than 10 percent of the total revenues to be shared. Third, and most depressing, the administration proposes to share these revenues without asking anything from the states in return.

We are in a dangerous period when many of the ground rules of the American system need to be overhauled. The states control most of these ground rules. They have been asleep at the social switch for too long. We cannot throw away the bargaining power represented by revenue sharing. To do so would be to miss a historic opportunity to negotiate essential changes in the way our states have been carrying on their public business.

If we begin sharing the proceeds of the federal income tax with states and cities without asking the states to pass their own income taxes, we really will have muffed it. The State of New Jersey, for instance, had damn well better change its basic revenue structure, as have most other states, to cure the inequities of the property tax, to get out from underneath the unfair distribution of aids by formulas which do not conform to present populations and their requirements.

I think we are likely to see some basic changes in the American revenue system during the next two years. The fight is on. The battle will center on the politicians' perception of what the country will take. President Nixon and his colleagues are quietly considering strong conditions to be attached to this aid, even though they have made public statements to the contrary.

But Moynihan's memo suggesting to the president "a period of benign neglect" on the racial issue was a giveaway of the going policy in Washington—which hovers between doing nothing at all that is controversial or trying to slip over something controversial on the public while saying as little as possible about it. Both alternatives are policies of neglect, and neither of them is benign.

If it had not been for both the action and the noise of the 1960s, we would not have won the very gains for blacks that Moynihan fears we will lose because of a reaction. Unless the noise level is up, social advancement never occurs.

Whether we like it or not, our social and political systems operate best when under tension. There are two roles for us to play in society. Starting from the middle we can go to the extreme of being nihilists or to the extreme of developing rigid establishmentarian characters. Most of us apparently have an instinct to work within reach of the middle ground, but we will follow alternating courses as we proceed. People like former Interior Secretary Udall and I held offices for a while within the system, to make it as responsive as possible; that was our role. However, as long as I am outside of the system, I am going to work the other side, which is intent on keeping the system under tension.

For example, I discovered during negotiations of racial issues in Newark that we were always at our best when under outside pressures to perform. Obviously I am talking about pressures and provocations hopefully short of violence. The use of violence as a pressure tactic will force even the most responsive and sensitive public official into a corner of defensive action, which becomes increasingly inflexible and establishmentarian. It was doubly helpful, therefore, to our officialdom in New Jersey when the blacks of Newark pressured us to perform by invoking the statutory and ethical considerations that brought us to their side. Their use of an Ohio court case threatening an injunction against state construction without affirmative action programs left Governor Richard J. Hughes and his administration no decent alternative but to accept the policy of integrating the building trades.

Ralph Nader may have developed one of our system's best new constitutional innovations, an equivalent of the ombudsman. But we can go a lot farther than Nader, who does not have a copyright on the business of keeping this system constantly under tension. I admire the ingenuity of our younger generation in finding those techniques, and I urge them to keep the system under tension for its own good and theirs.

This brings me to the youth of today and what they represent. Urban livability has been greatly improved over the last decade, despite some of the environmental degradation that we have seen. It has been improved by the addition of our younger generation. I do not know what has led that generation to take action, but it has been great. I could cite cases in which I would have liked to help mastermind a campaign that did not quite attain its goal, but by and large the youth movement has been great. Not because the young people possess superior wisdom but because they apparently have been born to the idea of a complex system. They were nurtured in it. The signals that wheel in on them have come from all 360 degrees of the compass.

I grew up in an age of specialization, in which one became an expert and then succeeded to the top. In this day, by comparison, I believe that the people who can live wholly and in the round will make out best. This seems to come instinctively to this young generation. In New Jersey, for example, we acted on this belief about the younger generation and imported 200 young people for our government during the summers. How they made that system move! We would give them an assignment for a whole summer, and they would come back twenty-four hours later to tell us it was finished; what should they do next? Our biggest problem was with their supervisors, who had not thought that far ahead and who usually underestimated the energy and ability of the young interns assigned to them.

There is something rare about today's younger generation and its energies. It ought to be recruited very quickly into the system.

One difficulty, however, is that the system excludes youth formally until age twenty-one. That is not serious for the white middle class. For the black and Puerto Rican, whose median age in the central cities is sixteen, it has meant that 70 percent have not been able to vote; the resultant natural restiveness explodes into the streets. Compare those people to the ethnic population whose median age is thirty-five to forty, about 80 to 90 percent of whom can vote and who can win municipal elections hands down. Until we change that part of the system and introduce the

younger generation, the whole apparatus will not operate successfully.

These few proposals on how to make urban life more livable—or
on how to make the life of each individual in our society more
livable—depend partly on our early willingness to see ourselves as
only single elements in an extraordinarily complex system. They
depend on an ability to fathom reaction, counterreaction,
strategy, counterstrategy, on into the third and fourth generation—of action far more complicated than some of the systems by
which we have conducted other operations. That instinct and that
self-discipline from within are essential.

Then, on the outside, some of the following formal changes are
necessary. The younger generation hopefully will not get bogged
down in the gimmickery or stultifying incrementalism of the last
ten or fifteen years. I would hope that youth will see clearly to
the jugular vein of the system, to its basic essentials, and then use
jujitsu or the lever of Archimedes—the longer the better—to pry
that system, to press it, to move it, and thus to shape it.

I would like to suggest one argument that might make me an
establishmentarian in the eyes of restless young people: the
longer I have lived with the system, the more clearly I see its
anarchic element. I see that as a function, a residual function,
of a lot of activities, not all of them so conspiratorial.

There *are* conspiracies. I have lived among the Mafia; I know
what it has done to Newark and other parts of New Jersey. I
have seen utility companies and other economic interests cap-
ture sectors of the system to use for their own purposes. I have
watched state legislators who have conspired to benefit the
narrow interests they represent.

But I recognize that the greatest problem is the system, which
has become so massive and complicated that it is beginning to
go out of control.

An element of that anarchy is extraordinarily healthy; another element is extraordinarily dangerous. At times it will require an assertiveness and a willingness to talk in nonconspira-
torial terms in order to take on the system, to see to that point

where the Wizard of Oz looks helpless behind the final machine. And then to declare at that point, with all available intelligence and humility, that we are willing to achieve more livable cities by attacking their fundamental maladies.

Are Capitalism and the Conservation of a Decent Environment Compatible?

Harry M. Caudill

I am addressing these remarks to my fellow students of this intriguing planet and to those voiceless unborn millions who must some day inhabit the wastelands this century is creating.

Symptoms of serious illness in our ecosystem abound on every hand. All who can discern the signs of our times must occasionally be depressed to melancholia and despair by the encroaching horror.

We are inflicting a doleful list of disasters on the only life-supporting planet known to astronomy:

Noxious emissions from automobile exhaust pipes, power plants, and factory stacks have buried our cities at the bottom of vast and oppressive atmospheric sewers.

Innumerable mills drain highly toxic acids and sludge into rivers and lakes.

Many municipalities pour sewage into rivers, compelling their neighbors downstream to drink chlorinated essence of urine.

These same municipalities too often dump mountains of trash into swamps or bury it in stinking mounds on every hand.

Tankers pump oily bilge into the oceans.

Petroleum escaping from undersea wells blackens beaches and kills marine life, as well as many birds.

Gigantic tankers are floating ecological disasters traveling about in quest of a place to happen.

Harry M. Caudill has gained a nationwide reputation by calling attention to the plight of the Appalachian land and people through his lectures and his book, Night Comes to the Cumberlands. *A lawyer and former Kentucky legislator, he vocally opposes destruction of the mountains by surface mining and supports severance taxes on extraction of mineral wealth, school reform, and justice for the neglected coal miners. He would use Appalachia's abundant riches for the people of the region, rather than for great absentee interests.*

Lumber corporations "harvesting" trees with bulldozers sometimes ruin the ecology of whole forests and destroy their capacity to regenerate the kind of timber resources the land once produced.

Agri-businessmen frequently drench their land with insecticides, pesticides, and fertilizers until the soil is dependent upon them, the ground water is rank with deadly concentrations of nitrates and phosphates, and new and ever more voracious strains of insects emerge to plague us.

Gargantuan feed lots, great pens where staggering numbers of cattle and hogs are kept for intensive feeding before slaughter, generate enormous quantities of manure—the sewage equivalent of large cities—that wastes into rivers to the ruinous deprivation of the land.

Manufacturers of automobiles, tin cans, glass bottles, and thousands of other products spew them out with no provision for recycling the scrap, thus cluttering the landscape with unimaginable quantities of junk.

Unsealed mines in a dozen states sluice sulfuric acid into streams on which strings of towns and cities are totally dependent for water.

Actually, the United States' massive degradation is only part of a worldwide debasement by which all the continents are systematically being robbed of the nutrients essential to the continuance of life, while the oceans simultaneously are choking with an accelerated flow of nutrients so vast that they cannot be assimilated. Thus man has become time's most traumatic geological force—a force that threatens to reduce the continents to deserts and the oceans to algae-ridden sumps.

The common theme running through this tapestry of ruin is an unbridled quest for economic advantage, a quest that becomes increasingly absurd because there can be no preeminence in the worldwide charnel house we are creating.

In the United States and throughout most of the world the economic system is impelled in a classic five-point cycle: *greed* produces *exploitation of other people* and *destruction of the land for its resources, pollution of the environment,* and finally, *monetary profit.* This system worked tolerably well for generations because the number of people was relatively small and the space and natural resources appeared to be inexhaustible. Now, however, the whole concept is losing validity with the twin realizations that the earth's natural resources are finite and that the procreative instinct, combined with modern medicine, can swamp the world with uncountable multitudes of human beings.

Under the prevailing ethics of the market place each corporation strives to manufacture its products at the lowest attainable cost and unload them on the public at the highest obtainable price. This inevitably results in a flow of unneeded—and frequently little tested—products into our homes and stomachs. The products are accompanied by seemingly endless misinformation, deceptions, and subtle suggestions of need, so that the consumer has scant basis for judgment as to what is safe or dangerous, desirable or pernicious.

The dominant attitude toward our mother earth continues to reflect the traditional savage frontier impulse to "gut, gouge, and git out!" From giant metal-mining companies down to small quarries, corporations routinely plunder the land and the communities dependent upon it, while making the smallest possible investment in social institutions. After pillaging the earth for resources to create products for sale to an unwitting public, the same corporations rid themselves of undesirable and dangerous residues by casting them onto or among their customers.

With a population of 205 million, we in the United States are much like the lady and her five suitors in Sir Richard Francis Burton's delightful nineteenth-century translation from *The Arabian Nights.* Everybody is defecating on everyone else and, despite the wails of protest, the practice continues. When hit, we emulate the outraged suitors and yell, "What nastiness is this?" Then we fling the odious substance onto someone else.

The situation was funny in Burton's fable, and generations have laughed at it; but we can see no mirth in it in the United States today. Indeed, if one insists on being amused, he may find himself laughing amid the skulls.

The madness that has brought us to our present untenable situation raises questions about man's fitness for survival. The technology of production expands constantly and, because production generates profits, the technology is vigorously applied. Simultaneously a huge reservoir of unused technology accumulates in the fields of air and water sanitation, waste abatement, and land regeneration. Such technology languishes because its application consumes profits. These dynamics are so potent that they threaten our very existence.

The issue thus posed transcends by far the conventional arguments for "conservation" and the "preservation of a decent environment." It brings us to a grim choice between survival and extinction. Survivalists believe that, regardless of costs, the insights of science must be employed to save the world's ecosystem as a functioning machine. The extinctionists murmur that there is no really serious problem and that, in any event, the contemplated costs are unthinkable. The contest between these points of view will dominate the next decade or two, and the outcome will determine whether life will continue into the twenty-first century.

We are led quite inevitably to consider whether capitalism and the conservation of a decent environment are compatible. Is the one impossible where the other holds sway?

To survive the sea of junk beneath which the capitalistic system is inundating us, will we be compelled to junk the system itself?

Because this symposium and book are originating in the Yale School of Forestry, I want to comment at length on the huge hardwood forest of the Cumberlands in the central Appalachian Mountains. It is so rich in flora, so varied in its life forms, so majestic in its natural beauty that its worth to mankind is inestimable. But our corporate system treats this marvelous forest and the minerals beneath its roots with a soulless rapacity that is unsurpassed in the annals of greed. Here capitalism has demonstrated its total contempt for the good earth, for the green that cloaks it, and for the creatures that dwell upon its face; it has achieved the supreme pollution of utter destruction. Unless our economic and political overlords change their attitudes toward it, the entire heart of this vast woodland will have been lost to the United States and the world long before the 1970s are gone.

When Europeans first viewed eastern Kentucky, it was a land of primordial splendor. Its web of life constituted an ecology of marvelous complexity and interdependency; it was indescribably ancient and, in some respects, remarkably frail.

Millions of visitors have reveled in the beauty and majesty of the Great Smokies, and most of the scientific attention that has been devoted to the Appalachians has centered in these high domes with their plunging streams, dense "laurel hells," and stately groves. Other than professional botanists and foresters, few are aware that the richest expression of the great eastern deciduous forest of North America was found in the Cumberland Plateau region in eastern Kentucky, rather than in the loftier and more venerable Smokies. Indeed, the finest forest in the world's temperate zones was found there, exceeding all other areas in the variety of trees, in age and size attained, and in the almost limit- less quantity and diversity of the low-growing ground cover above their roots.

This vast and remarkable woodland is of a character known to ecologists as "mixed mesophytic forest"—that is, midway be- tween wet and dry, and implying a moderate climate and a rich vegetation in a well-drained habitat that is protected from ex- cessive exposure to burning sun and drying wind.

All of these environmental characteristics are found in full mea- sure in the Kentucky Cumberlands. In July the thermometer rarely climbs above 90 degrees; in January it seldom sinks to zero. Rainfall amounts to nearly 50 inches annually, more than in any other part of the United States except the rain forest of Oregon and Washington. The ridges are gentle, and ages-long erosion by wind and water has carved their slopes into deep coves and capped their crests with picturesque crags of sandstone. They reach their highest elevation on the southern border in the Big Black Mountain, but even here, at 4,400 feet above sea level, they fall short of the arctic air that produces the balds that dot the Smokies. In the moist, warm, protected coves a benevolent nature set the stage for the highest development of that type of vege-

tation botanists have termed "the deciduous forest of the
Northern Temperate Climatic Zone."

In no other forest in the Northern Hemisphere can we count so
many kinds of trees; the total number of species exceeds a hundred. Nowhere else on earth do the hillsides blaze with such a rich
tapestry of color in the autumn, each specie assuming its own
particular shade of scarlet or gold or plum, of mahogany, rose,
orange or yellow—all glowing against the deep, dark evergreen of
the pines, hemlocks, rhododendrons, and laurels. Nowhere else on
our planet is the spring so fragrant and gay from March to June as
one tree and shrub after another comes into bloom.

Geologic upheaval occurred there long before our modern
forest evolved. And long before that upheaval the land was
covered by shallow seas fringed with a rank growth of tree-size
club mosses and gigantic ferns. In those remote ages litter from
the swampy forests accumulated in the shallow waters and
formed the organic deposits that were to be turned, by time and
the weight of later sediments, into the potent mineral we call
coal. Finally the weight of accumulating sediments became too
great for the crust to bear. The earth buckled, rearing the Appalachians far above the continental floor. The long ridges that form
the backbone of the Cumberlands and Alleghanies were a part of
this vast Appalachian uplift. Later and more gentle uplifts per-
petuated the mountainous character of the land, which otherwise
would long ago have been worn down by the incessant action of
water.

For more than 200 million years this land has been here above
the seas, relatively unchanged except for alternating cycles of
erosion and uplift. In this immense era of stability nature perfected the forest that astounded the first white explorers, a woodland so venerable that if one could enter a time machine and
explore time's abyss he would find growing here trees closely
resembling those we can see today—but 70 million years before
man stood erect anywhere on the planet.

During the early part of the geologic period known as the Tertiary the Rocky Mountains were low hills, and even the arctic
regions were blessed with mild temperatures. The trees of the

Cumberlands grew far westward across North America. They put down their roots along the shores of Greenland and northward into Alaska. Then, over land bridges that have long since vanished, they reached northeastern Asia and advanced southward into China.

Rock fossils tell us the story of these trees and of the fragile ground cover that grew in their ancient shade. The imprint of sycamore and maple leaves has been found along the front of the Rockies in Montana, Colorado, and the Dakotas; their track remains in Greenland and northern Canada. As impressive as these stone traces of forests that rose and died are the forest survivals that have persisted to our own time. In central Appalachia and in eastern China the tulip tree grows beside sassafras, sweet gum, spicewood, and magnolias. Nowhere else in today's world, except in eastern North America and eastern China, are these species found. Many of the flowers and ferns beneath them are common to both regions.

But there were forces at work to reduce the forest in the same eons when it reached its greatest magnitude and splendor. Twenty or thirty million years ago, and again only a million or so years ago, the land rose from northwestern Canada to New Mexico and the Rockies of today were thrust up to their towering heights. They acted as a barrier to the moisture-laden winds from the Pacific, and the rain and snow fell on the western slopes of the ragged new ridges. The central stretches of the continent became too dry to support trees; they became a grassland, and the forest retreated to the east where rain from the Atlantic provided moisture for its perpetuation.

Slowly the north turned cold. The deciduous trees retreated southward for thousands of miles and were replaced by firs and spruces moving down from frigid mountaintops. The deciduous forest was restricted to eastern America south of Canada and north of the subtropics. Similar changes in Asia restricted that portion of the forest to eastern China.

Then came the frigid Pleistocene, with its continental glaciers that began grinding down from the north about a million years ago. At their greatest extent the glaciers covered all of New

England, reached the southern tip of Illinois, spread across Indiana and Ohio and most of Pennsylvania. The gargantuan shields of sliding ice destroyed all vegetation in their path, but they inched forward so slowly that northern species of trees managed to survive by seeding ever southward in front of the glacial margin. Thus spruce and fir came to stand beside magnolia and pawpaw, and to this day they are found as "glacial relics" on the highest peaks of the Smokies.

At last the glaciers retreated northward, leaving in their wake a bleak, shattered land. Everywhere the glaciers had dumped immense loads of pulverized rock—in drifts, in heaps, and in ground sheets. No "soil" remained in the path of the glaciers. The paper-thin sheet of nutrient-rich, humus-filled material that had been built up through millions of years had been completely dissipated in the rubble heaps. Not until the arrival of modern "civilized" man with his diesel engines and bulldozers would the North American continent again experience such thoroughgoing devastation.

Climates were much colder south of the ice sheet than they are now, but they were not frigid enough to kill vegetation far beyond the glacial rim. In the protected valleys and deep coves of Appalachia and the Ozarks the deciduous forest survived, to serve as a huge storehouse of seeds to reclothe the naked land.

Some plants are exceedingly adaptable and, as the ice withdrew, they followed closely in its wake. The first to pursue the receding ice shield were those plants of northern origin: the spruce and fir, the bunchberry and bead lilly. These hardy pioneers began the infinitely slow process of rebuilding soil in the rubble heaps and on the bare rocks, preparing the way for other plants that must have a more luxuriant environment for their survival. As temperatures climbed, white pine, sugar maple, and yellow birch crept out of the hills to replace the spruce and fir. Then the oaks, the beeches and tulip trees could also move northward again.

Throughout the long, bleak millennia of the Ice Age the ancient forest of the Cumberland plateau survived in all its infinite variety. Protected by a labyrinth of coves and valleys, its trees were ready to seed northward and northwestward to establish new woodlands. However, not all of the species could tolerate pioneer environments—the drought, the alternating extremes of heat and cold, and the raw abrasive characteristics of the deeply scarred land. Some, especially the white basswood and the yellow buckeye, demand rich humus and the protection of a long-established forest; so they remained in the Cumberlands and in the lessening hills to the south. Others could endure cold but not drought; so the beech, sugar maple, hemlock, and yellow birch spread northward into New England, then across Canada and into Wisconsin. Others could tolerate drought as well as cold; so the oaks and hickories moved both northwestward and northward.

Not all of them could make it to the western limits of the deciduous forest, where the prairies begin. The chestnut oaks dropped out in Indiana. The tulip poplar demanded rich soil and much moisture when it left its ancient home; it could travel as far as Indiana, southern Michigan, and the eastern limits of Illinois, where it survives today in only the most luxuriant habitats. The forest that reached the northwestern limits of the deciduous preserves contains fewer than a fifth of the species found in the Cumberland heartland.

A new geologic force has obtruded upon the forest—mechanized man. His efforts at "development" threaten to eradicate that which the glaciers spared. Unlike the great ice sheets, man can go anywhere; no flower or fern or tree, or any creature that shelters in their shade, can escape him. He is a living cataclysm. The question now is not whether the age-old forest can ever again spread to new regions, but simply whether it can manage to survive, even in its ancient mountain fastnesses.

The Indians treated the forest of the Cumberlands with supreme reverence. It was frequented by the Cherokee and numerous lesser tribes, who harmed it as little as shadows cast by the clouds.

The white men who drove them out decimated the forest, clearing huge areas for cattle pastures and the endless "new grounds" on which their agriculture depended. After the turn of this century coal mining began, and tunnels were thrust into hundreds of hillsides. At one time 55,000 men were boring into the Cumberlands, propping up countless miles of sagging sandstone with timbers from the hills above their heads.

However, the wounded forest—with the exception of the chestnut tree—survived in all its multitudinous forms down to our own time. (The noble chestnut perished from an imported blight that swept the nation in 1929.) The almost endless catalogue of plants that made the hills and valleys so distinctive were there, ready to reconstitute the forest in all its magnificence when time and the prudence of man could combine to permit it.

In the 1950s a vast human exodus flowed out of the hills into northern cities. The old mining industry, with its dependence on thousands of laborers, collapsed. Machines replaced men in the tunnels, and strip mining developed on a large scale. The deserted areas quickly reverted to new forests. The open fields disappeared under a choking growth of young trees. In a strange silence amid vacant, decaying houses along hundreds of creeks the old grandeur of the Cumberlands began to return.

But this forest, which had passed through so many trials during the vast span of its history, was to face its most devastating crisis at the hands of men digging coal with explosives, bulldozers, and power shovels. At this hour the mountains and their vegetation are under the most deadly and systematic assault any portion of the North American land ever has suffered.

In the Cumberlands three to five veins of coal run through each hill, and the demand for it appears to be insatiable. It generates our electric power, smelts our metals, and provides medicines and fertilizers. The cheapest way to get it out of the ground is by surface mining. Behind the rumble of exploding dynamite the bulldozers shove their way along the contours of the hills, spreading a wake of devastation that can scarcely be believed. The mind boggles at the immensity and completeness of the ruin.

Generally the first coal seam to be worked is the one nearest the base of the hill. The contour cut produces a great notch or flat bench at the level of the vein. The earth and its living organisms are simply thrust aside by the massive machines and the shattering blasts. The rock and dirt above the coal are pushed down the slope, and an abrupt man-made cliff rears sheer and sullen from thirty to ninety feet in height. A serpentine expanse of glittering carbon stretches behind the roaring Euclids and Caterpillars, and after the coal is loosened by new explosions, the power shovels lift it into trucks that speed their twenty-five-ton cargoes to the railroads.

After the base of the hill has been reduced in this manner, the process is repeated at the next level. Sometimes the top of a mountain is blasted away, and the ancient crags and their oaks are rolled into the hollows. Sharp weather-carved mountains become man-made mesas.

In Breathitt County, Kentucky, a whole range is being dismembered. Layer by layer the mountains are being cut down and the spoil pushed into the valleys. The labyrinth of hills and valleys is being reduced to a jumble of broken rock, slate, shale, and yellow subsoil. Under all this ruin lies the corpse of a forest.

Kentucky has a reclamation law; after the last of the hardwoods, ferns, and flowers has been rooted out and buried, men walk over the dead acidulous earth scattering fescue and lespedeza seeds. In a few instances hydro-seeders spray water, straw, fertilizer, and seeds across the rock-strewn jumble. Later a few hundred pine seedlings are planted on each acre. Then the land is certified as "reclaimed" and, with awesome finality, is forgotten.

In the meantime the inhabitants of the valleys take flight. Massive erosion from spoil banks sends thick sheets of mud onto their lawns and croplands and into the channels of creeks. Wells go dry or become highly mineralized. Ugliness marks their communities, and people refuse to stay in such hideous surroundings. A million Kentuckians have fled the hills since 1950. Strip mining has been one of the prime causes of their exodus.

Much of the land is owned by coal companies, who bought it cheaply in the 1880s. The mineral rights on practically all the remaining land are owned by the same companies under deeds that sever the title to the minerals from that of the surface. Kentucky's highest court has ruled that the owner of the minerals may "recover" them by any means he deems necessary or convenient, including stripping [*Martin v. Kentucky Oak Mining Co.,* 429 SW 2d (Ky.), p. 395]. This court of justice has declared that,

although stripping totally destroys the land, the mining company
has no obligation to make restitution to the farmer who owns the
trees and topsoil.

Can there be any wonder that the region is synonymous with
poverty and dejection?

Thus the destruction of a broad territory has been given lawful
sanction, and while men talk of saving the environment, the ruin
spreads like an obscene cancer. Two hundred thousand acres of
eastern Kentucky forest land have already been ruined. In all of
Appalachia a million acres have been similarly devastated, and the
coal market is now so strong that the giant machines seldom rest
by day or night.

Who are these destroyers of this ancient part of our terrestrial
heritage? Are they madmen turned out of insane asylums? Are
they Bolsheviks who have found a way of destroying the United
States by plundering her land?

They are, in fact, some of the nation's most respected names.
They include U.S. Steel, Bethlehem Steel, Ford Motor Company,
Continental Oil, Occidental Petroleum, Republic Steel, Georgia
Power, American Electric Power, and Uncle Sam himself operating through the Tennessee Valley Authority (TVA). Many of
the great interests that mine, transport, and consume coal are
engaged in this gigantic rape.

According to Ferdinand Lundberg's noteworthy study of the
United States power structure, *The Rich and the Super-Rich,* the
fantastically wealthy Mellon family holds billions in their coffers.
He says that the family controls Bethlehem Steel, and a subsidiary of Bethlehem Steel owns about 40,000 acres in four
eastern Kentucky counties. This land is dark with second-growth
hardwoods, and much of it has been deep-mined. But 8 million
tons of high-grade metallurgical coal remain in the outcrop, the
narrow border of coal at the outside of the hill that subterranean
mining procedures cannot "recover." Bethlehem Steel has ignored
the protests of the National Audubon Society, the World Wildlife
Fund, the Izaak Walton League, the Sierra Club, and the pleas of
hundreds of just plain Americans. Those 8 million tons will have a
market worth of $44 million when fed into Bethlehem's furnaces.

The cost of those dollars to the nation will be desolate wastelands stretching across the middle of Appalachia. The Mellons will have added a few more unneeded millions to their hoard. Bethlehem will continue its massive shipments of cheap steel to foreign countries (among them the Soviet Union), and several thousand new Appalachian migrants will have fled into the slums of Cleveland and Chicago.

Bethlehem's operation began on Millstone Creek in a week when Mrs. Paul Mellon was interviewed at Upperville, Virginia, at one of her five spacious homes. Her husband and his kinsmen had given away $700 million, including much largesse to Yale. She conducted the reporter through her lovely garden, speaking with pride of its flowers and shrubs.

Since then Mrs. Mellon's garden has passed through another season of growth and bloom, but Millstone Valley will bloom no more. As the local newspaper has reported, "Millstone Creek is dead."

Thus there are two kinds of gardens that our rich masters create. The one is truly beautiful, with its precious plants and blooms surrounding stately houses and shaded drives. The other will be inhabited by people like you and me, and by those who will carry our genes in the aftertime, and consists of tumbled wastes like those described in the opening verses of Genesis.

Corporations headquartered in New York and Philadelphia hold the destiny of the Cumberlands in their hands. I have no doubt that—despite the golden rhetoric emanating from Washington's federal cave of winds—this forest and other mineral-bearing lands in the nation are doomed. You and I will protest, but the destruction will continue. We have voices, but the corporate directors have power. We are serfs; they are the masters.

The attitude of our capitalist overlords was clearly expressed by James D. Reilly, a vice president of Consolidated Coal Company, in a speech at Pittsburgh on May 8, 1969:

> The conservationists who want strip-miners to restore land are stupid idiots, Socialists, and Commies who don't know what they are talking about. I think it is our bounden duty

to knock them down and subject them to the ridicule they deserve.

It is remarkable how much times have changed since the year 1000, and yet how much they have remained the same. In that distant era the barons and their ladies lived in moated castles, surrounded by retainers and supported by multitudes of toiling serfs. The countries were run by their feudal elites. No one consulted the serfs or listened to their occasional entreaties.

A millennium of advancing technology has elevated living standards for all, and the lords of the land now live in different surroundings. But the barons are still with us, and they exercise most of the prerogatives of a royal class. The new royalty consists of the corporate power structure, and the serfs are the people who work for them and pay the taxes that keep the system going.

Sometimes the serfs strike or march in protest. They petition lawmakers and write letters to editors; but make no mistake, the power is in the board rooms. A telephone call from S. S. Corts, president of Bethlehem Steel, to a governor or the president of the United States is likely to achieve more than an entreaty signed by many thousands of ordinary one-vote citizens. The thing that distinguishes serfs and masters in the modern U.S.A. is the power to make decisions, and that power is where the weight of unlimited millions of dollars focuses. It is not with the individual citizens, no matter how concerned, intelligent, and vocal they may be.

For this reason the Fords continue to pollute the River Rouge as they have for sixty years. The Ford family fortune is gigantic, as befits a tribe which has poured gigantic quantities of wastes into our air and water. To date they have polluted with impunity.

However, no polluters can exceed the Rockefellers. They have turned the Garden State into a sink of nauseous gases from the refineries of Rockefeller-dominated Standard Oil of New Jersey. But Rockefellers are clever as well as rich. They distribute largesse among the serfs and hire clever propagandists to cozen and mislead them. Consequently, Rockefellers govern a growing list of states. From the top of Rockefeller Center they can gaze down into the filthy canyons of a city that their companies have done much to render squalid and hideous. They can yacht in oceans that their tankers have helped to turn rancid with their wastes.

And, of course, the exploits of the $7 billion Dupont clan are worthy of note. Their grip on once lovely Delaware is sure, and their chemical wastes have damned land, air, and water alike.

These examples illustrate the awesome power of the polluters. They would like to see the country clean and lovely; but making it that way will cost immense sums, and the polluters are in the business of accumulating—not expending—money. They will be happy to see the United States cleaned up, if the serfs will pay the bill.

Keep in mind that Richard Nixon and the fifty governors are merely foremen who run the economic ranch for such polluters and destroyers as General Motors, Ford, Occidental Petroleum, Continental Oil, Gulf Oil, Standard Oil of New Jersey, U.S. Steel, and practically the whole roster of United States industrial might. Such foremen are carried into office on cash gifts from their economic masters who exercise their subtle but effective control over both parties. Almost every truly powerful "establishment" figure in Congress is a steadfast servant of the rich.

Our masters—like the barons of feudal England before them— are too big to restrain. When Lyndon Johnson talked of a war on poverty or Richard Nixon spoke of a campaign against environmental decline, each had to resort to broad generalities. The dynamics of the power structure prevent the singling out of culprits who create poverty and ugliness. To do so would spark an uprising among the barons, while the serfs would remain quiescent or unresponsive. Under three United States presidents I have tried to entice a secretary of the interior into eastern Kentucky to look at the devastation of strip mining, but none has dared to come. I thought his high office would dramatize a national concern for the desperate plight of Appalachia's expiring hills. Each secretary expressed a sincere personal concern, but none would brave the wrath of the barons. So the hills died friendless, and the ruin widened, as it still does.

Brave to foolhardiness is the politician who will beard a Mellon, a Rockefeller, or a Dupont. Prisons are made for serfs; mansions are constructed for lords. Every day Americans go to penitentiaries for petty thefts. But when a roomful of belted knights from General Electric and Westinghouse fixed prices and defrauded the government of hundreds of millions of dollars, they were fined and given short jail sentences—most of which are suspended.

In my opinion our present system of government can never cope with the horrendous problems of our deteriorating environment. It has come down to us as a Rube Goldberg contraption consisting of one federal government, fifty states, 3,500 counties, and an indescribable tangle of 76,000 other governmental units. This jungle can absorb—and waste—tax money as sand soaks up water, but its very complexity and immensity induce near paralysis. At every turn opponents of change baffle and retard undertakings that deserve the highest priority. In such a swamp implementation of reform programs is an exhausting nightmare experience. Huge undertakings generally accomplish little and, out of bewilderment and frustration, the public loses interest and withdraws its support. Thus, at a time when we must strive to save ourselves, our principal instrument of survival is archaic, overgrown, inefficient, and uninspired. I can think of no major problem of war or peace with which this governmental monstrosity is able to deal successfully.

If the needs of our whole society could be served, if we could escape the baronial restraints that reduce our democratic system to near immobility, we could enact and strictly enforce a federal law to save the Appalachians and the other mineral fields of the United States. It would:

1. Outlaw strip mining where prompt and total restoration of the land and its water and vegetation is impossible. This would stop the practice altogether in Appalachia.
2. Permit stripping only where prompt and total restoration of the land to its original contour and natural utility can be accomplished. Topsoil on the plains can be scraped back and saved. The underlying strata can be dug out and segregated. After the mineral is lifted out, the strata can go back to their

natural order. The surface can be smoothed and treated with limestone and fertilizers and can be made useful again. Such procedures are routine in England, Germany, and Czechoslovakia, but they are rarely employed in America the Beautiful.

3. Levy a substantial severance tax on the extraction of all minerals. This money would be devoted to reclamation—insofar as reclamation is possible—of the 4 million acres of strip-mined land and the 10,000 miles of ruined streams that are making much of the United States as hideous as the pockmarked face of a corpse.

We have or can acquire the capacity to restore our land and air, to preserve our rivers and seas, to safeguard our mountains, to limit our numbers—in short, to assure the survival of our planet. But my optimism about the likelihood that we will do so is restrained.

I fear that greed and indifference will continue to hold sway in the nation's boardrooms, where not even life will outweigh the lust for profits. I am afraid we are headed into a new politics of pious gesture and bold rhetoric, dramatized by occasional visits to stinking lakes, the planting of a few trees, and the dedication now and then of a new sewage treatment plant. As one who was born during the Return to Normalcy, grew up under the New Deal, went to war for the Four Freedoms, was mustered out under the Fair Deal, marched in the Great Crusade, fared forth to the New Frontier, and enlisted in the Great Society, I have developed certain reservations about the sincerity of officials who proclaim grand new goals.

I come from eastern Kentucky, one of the world's richest resource regions and certainly a primary ecological disaster area of the United States. I have seen capitalism at work there through many painful years. I have seen one of the richest lands on earth acrawl with the poorest people in the nation, where illiteracy runs to one-fourth of the adults, and the very name of the region equates with poverty. I have seen pipelines lacing the land to carry out rivers of oil and gas, and since infancy my sleep has been disturbed by the rumbling of endless coal drags and lumber trains. I have seen hordes of people lining up for food stamps and the dole, and swarms of school children in tattered clothes trudging past the offices of the United States' richest corporations on their way to tumbledown schoolhouses perched above junk-choked streams.

In addition to the poorest white people in this country, my neighbors have long included the two most prosperous investor-owned corporations in the United States—the Penn-Virginia Company and Kentucky River Coal. Each clears, after taxes, sixty-one cents out of every dollar, and pays out as dividends 45 percent of its gross receipts. I have seen legislators and presidents tax meager salaries and bread, clothing, and medicine while granting an astonishing tax immunity to these same corporations. And I have read the proud boast of the president of Penn-Virginia, "We carry practically all of our income down to net."

Here we have the reality that looms up like a dark mountain—the reality of a multitude of uncertain and crisis-ridden governments, and virtually all of them dependent upon and subservient to the economic barons; a reality of ever-darkening cities, reeking rivers, putrefying lakes, dying mountains and burgeoning populations.

Albert Schweitzer once wrote, "Man has lost the capacity to foresee and to forestall. He will end by destroying the earth." His grim prophecy is certain to occur unless this generation of serfs finds some way of rising against their overlords, the globe-girdling corporate litter kings, and instituting somehow and quickly an international land ethic for the nurture, enhancement, and conservation of the earth. In short, a whole generation must become militant and vocal advocates—not only for themselves but for the unborn multitudes who have a right to be heard but cannot speak. This is the urgent necessity of survival. Without such a land ethic, without a regeneration of the spirit in matters relating to the land, beginning here and spreading across the world, there will be no future.

Such a regeneration would be truly revolutionary, and revolutions are extremely hard to bring off. The earth is a generous mother and will provide for all her children, if they will populate her with prudence and treat her with restraint. The capitalistic system has yet to demonstrate that it is capable of such restraint. Nor, for that matter has any other system. For example, the Russians under Communism have devastated and polluted on a scale approaching our own.

As I listen to murmurings of concern, I like to suppose that I hear the faint beginning of a revolt and of a new politics of survival, a politics that will say frankly to capitalism: "You claim to live by the motto 'produce or perish.' Now we demand that you produce a decent environment in the lands you dominate or make way for a new system of economics and a new order of values. Goods alone are not enough!"

If such a revolt comes, it will fight entrenched institutions of great age and wealth, institutions that now wield practically every instrument of power—economic, political, and social. All of these weapons will be exercised with cunning and tenacity to delay change and to preserve the doomed and polluted present.

And so I leave you to ponder a paraphrase from the Right— from Barry Goldwater's 1964 presidential nomination acceptance speech:* Moderation in the cause of survival is no virtue! Extremism in the cause of survival is no vice!

*Goldwater said: "Moderation in defense of liberty is no virtue. Extremism in defense of liberty is no vice."

This Generation's Strategy to Save the Environment

Gaylord Nelson

In the nearly forty years since Franklin D. Roosevelt said in his first inaugural address that "this great nation will endure as it has endured, will revive and will prosper," our economy has soared to levels that no one in the 1930s could have imagined. In these past four decades we have become the wealthiest nation on earth by almost any measure of production and consumption.

As the economic boom and the postwar population explosion continued to break all records, a national legend developed: with science and technology as its tools, the private-enterprise system could accomplish anything.

We assumed that, if private enterprise could turn out more automobiles, airplanes, and TV sets than all the rest of the world combined, somehow it could create a transportation system that would work. If we were the greatest builders in the world, we need not worry about our poor and about the planning and building of our cities. With enough technology and enough profit, private enterprise would manage that just fine.

In short, we assumed that, if private enterprise could be such a spectacular success in the production of goods and services, it could do our social planning for us, too; set our national priorities; shape our social system; and even establish our individual aspirations.

In the 1960s the era of technological innovation and new affluence marched on to levels unprecedented in the history of man. It

Gaylord Nelson, a U.S. Senator from Wisconsin, is particularly well known as an environmentalist. His legislative accomplishments include an amendment to the antipoverty program putting to work unemployed and elderly people on conservation projects, the 1969 passage of legislation which will lead to the establishment of water quality standards on pesticides, the inclusion of major rivers in the National Wild and Scenic Rivers System, and the establishment of automobile safety standards and tire safety and quality standards. Before election to the U.S. Senate, he served two terms as Wisconsin's governor, and prior to that was a three-term state senator. In September 1969 Senator Nelson proposed and was cochairman of the nationwide environmental effort, Earth Day, in 1970.

was the decade when man walked on the moon; when medical magic transplanted the human heart; when the computer's mechanical wizardry became a part of daily life; and when— instead of "a chicken in every pot"—the national aim seemed to be two cars in every garage, a summer home, a color television set, and a vacation in Europe.

From the small farmers and small merchants of the last century we had become the "consumer society," with science and technology as the New Testament and the Gross National Product as the Holy Grail.

One might have thought we would have emerged triumphantly from the 1960s with a shout: "Bring on the next decade!"

We have not. For in addition to the other traumatic national and international events, the 1960s produced another kind of "top-of-the-decade" list. It was a decade in which the darkening cloud of pollution began seriously degrading the thin envelope of air around the globe; when pesticides and unrestricted waste disposal threatened the productivity of all the oceans of the world; when virtually every lake, river, and watershed in the United States began to show the distressing symptoms of being overloaded with polluting materials.

These pivotal events have begun to warn the nation of a disturbing new paradox: the mindless pursuit of quantity is destroying—not enhancing—the opportunity to achieve quality in our lives. In the words of the American balladeer, Pete Seeger, we have found ourselves "standing kneedeep in garbage, throwing rockets at the moon."

Cumulatively, "progress, American style" adds up each year to 200 million tons of smoke and fumes, 8 million junked cars, 40 million tons of waste paper, and 76 billion bottles and cans. It also means bulldozers gnawing away at the landscape to make room for more unplanned expansion, more leisure time but less open space in which to spend it, and so much reckless progress that we face even now a dangerously polluted environment.

As one measure of the rate of consumption that demands our resources and creates our vast wastes, it has been estimated that all the American children born in just one year will use up 200 million pounds of beef during their lifetimes.

To provide electricity for our air conditioners, a Kentucky hillside is strip-mined. To provide gasoline for our automobiles, the ocean floor is drilled for oil. To provide sites for our second homes, the shore of a pristine lake is subdivided.

The unforeseen (or ignored) consequences of an urbanizing, affluent, mobile, more populous society have poisoned, scarred, and polluted what once was a beautiful land "from sea to shining sea."

Today it can be said that there is no clear air left in the United States. The last vestige of pure air was near Flagstaff, Arizona; it disappeared six years ago.

It can be said, also, that there is no river or lake in the United States that has not been affected by the pervasive wastes of our society. On Lake Superior, the last clean Great Lake, a mining company is dumping 60,000 long tons of iron-ore process wastes directly into the lake every day.

Tomorrow? Responsible scientists have predicted that accelerating rates of air pollution could become so serious by the 1980s that many people may be forced on the worst days to wear breathing helmets to survive outdoors.

It has also been predicted that in twenty years man will live in domed cities.

S. Dillon Ripley, Secretary of the Smithsonian Institution, has estimated that in twenty-five years somewhere between 75 and 80 percent of all the species of living animals will be extinct.

Paul Ehrlich, eminent California ecologist, and many other scientists predict the end of the oceans as a productive resource within the next fifty years unless pollution is stopped. The United States provides an estimated one-third to one-half of the industrial pollution of the sea. It is especially ironic that, even as we pollute the sea, we hope its resources can be used to feed tens of millions of hungry people.

As in the great depression, America is again faced with a crisis that has to do with material things, but it is an entirely different sort of dilemma. In effect, America has bought environmental disaster on a national installment plan: acquire affluence now and let future generations pay the price. Trading away the future is a high price to pay for an electric swizzle stick or for a car with greater horsepower. But then, the environmental consequences have never been included on the labels.

We have gotten into this predicament, not by design, but by default. Somehow the environmental problems have mushroomed upon us from the blind side of our existence—although even decades ago a few lonely voices were warning of trouble to come.

Now, I think, a great awakening is under way. We have begun to recognize that our security is again threatened, not from the outside but from the inside, not by our enemies but by ourselves.

A Gallup poll taken for the National Wildlife Federation in 1969 revealed that 51 percent of all persons interviewed were deeply disturbed about the grim tide of pollution.

Growing student environmental concern is a striking new development. A college student-attitude poll, conducted in the fall of 1969 by the American Council on Education, found that 89.9 percent of all male freshmen believed the federal government should be more involved in the control of pollution. And another Gallup poll published in late December 1969 found that the control of air and water pollution is fast becoming a new student cause, with students placing this issue very high on a list of areas where they feel changes must be made.

Our young people are now questioning—and beginning to reject—a "progress" that means obliterating the countryside with an endless highway building program that has the apparent aim of enabling us to drive from coast to coast without meeting a stoplight. Or filling San Francisco Bay for industrial development. Or threatening to subject the whole nation to a new round of sonic booms to save a few hours' travel time with the SST. Or littering the camping areas of the country with "disposable" paper sleeping bags for the ultimate in convenience in the consumer society.

Add to the concern of youth that of the laboring man, who must frequently live in the shadows of the spewing smokestacks of industry . . . the commuter who inches in spurts along an expressway . . . the housewife who pays too much for products that begin to fall apart too soon . . . and the black man living alongside the noisy, polluted truck routes through the central-city ghetto.

Across this broad spectrum of American society there is a disgust; a fear; a rising anger; a yearning for participation, information, and action. In New Jersey a meeting to form a town conservation group attracted 500 persons. At the University of Michigan in the fall of 1969 a meeting to begin planning an environmental teach-in drew so many students that the organizers had to find a larger hall. A mention on a national television program of Senate apprehension for the dangers facing Everglades National Park in southern Florida brought my office hundreds of letters stressing citizen concern for this priceless national resource. In Washington a daily average of 150 constituent requests on environmental questions is coming from congressional members to the Legislative Reference Service, the research arm of Congress.

A sense of a developing movement for a new quality in American life is building with incredible speed and spontaneity. In the freshest participatory-democracy idea in our country today, citizen environmental watchdog arms of local government have sprouted in 571 communities in seven northeastern states. Citizens and conservation groups are meeting assaults on the environment with court suits, and more and more often they are winning. In some of our cities black youth gangs have cleaned up ghetto blocks at night and have followed up by writing anonymous letters to editors to report their deeds.

On the other side of the spectrum, in conservative Orange County south of Los Angeles outraged citizens and public officials have been vigorously protesting massive development plans that would alter forever the natural ecology of Newport Bay.

Earth Day 1970 saw nationwide environmental events led by student initiative but involving the ever-expanding range of environmental interests in this society. The response to Earth Day was overwhelming. Some 2,000 colleges and universities, 10,000 high schools and grade schools representing millions of students, and several thousand communities participated in what may prove to be one of the most exciting and significant grassroots efforts in the history of this country.

More than any other single event, Earth Day presented specific information on environmental problems in every community; it drew the issues, stimulated plans for action, and demonstrated the widespread national concern for a livable world.

This is a new and pervasive concern. One can sense it all across the land. This new politics of ecological concern makes me believe for the first time that we can wage a successful war to save our environment.

But make no mistake; it will be a long and tough political fight that will require a national commitment on a scale comparable to those we have made for the national defense and for putting man on the moon. Are we willing, for example, to start soon to commit $25 to $30 billion a year—and in the future $40 to $50 billion annually—to problems of the environment? Or isn't this issue as important as our very questionable involvement in Vietnam at a cost of tens of billions of dollars a year?

Just what are some of the philosophical commitments, some of the costs, some of the sacrifices we will have to make to preserve this planet as a livable world?

Surely as a fundamental first step it will require the evolution of an attitude, a philosophy, an ethic emphasizing our interdependence with nature and rejecting the prevailing philosophy of Western civilization that man can dominate the earth while ignoring the works and forces of nature.

It will require a transition from a society that pursues profit and material goods at any price to one that concerns itself as much with the well-being of present and future generations as it does with bigness and abundance. It will mean establishing quality on a par with quantity as an aim of American life.

If we are going to do more than maintain the status quo, waging war on our environmental problems will involve adopting new policies. Quite frankly, those policies will interfere with what many have considered their right to use and abuse our air, water, and land resources just because that is what man has done throughout history.

Getting the job done will involve responsibilities on the part of the individual, on the part of local and state government, and on the part of the nation itself. At each level significant steps have to be taken to protect the environment.

Nationally, the initial basic steps that must be taken include establishing the following major new environmental policies.

A national land-use policy. We must establish a national land-use policy with enough teeth to stop the kind of development for industry, commerce, highways, and housing that recklessly drains and fills our wetlands, destroying wildlife habitat and polluting coastal and inland waters; that carves up our inland lake and coastal shorelines, eliminating a vital national asset from public use; that brings massive land erosion in urbanizing areas, silting our rivers and lakes; that devastates whole regions with scrape-up-and-get-out strip-mining operations. For strip mining alone we have laid open lands equivalent to a 1.5 million-mile strip 100 feet wide in this country.

A national policy to eliminate the ghetto. We need a new national policy and top priority for the elimination of the ghetto, where the worst environment in the world exists. There, millions of people suffer the greatest noise, the worst air pollution, the fewest parks, the worst housing, the worst traffic jams. I intend to introduce in the Senate very shortly a proposal for a Community Environment Service to create jobs for the poor and to greatly boost efforts to restore the livability of our decaying cities. Environment is all of America and its problems. It is the rats in the ghetto. It is a hungry child in a land of affluence. It is housing that is not worthy of the name, neighborhoods not fit to inhabit. The battle to save our cities and end the divisiveness that still splits this country will not be won in Vietnam.

A national policy on air and water quality. We must establish a national policy on air and water quality that requires all governmental units and all industries and municipalities to comply with the highest state of the art in treating their wastes. We must also require the installation without delay of new, more effective pollution-control equipment as it is developed.

A national policy on recycling wastes. We must establish a national policy to recycle wastes, vastly expanding research and development to find economic uses for the wastes of the society, making them valuable "resources out of place." A top priority should be developing reusable or degradable bottles, cans, and jars and outlawing the "throwaways" that are littering the countryside and increasing the costs of solid-waste disposal. To this end I have introduced legislation, the Packaging Pollution Control Act of 1970, which would establish a disposal charge on all packaging materials, to be paid by the manufacturer. This charge would be scaled to reflect the environmental quality of each package and its effect on solid-waste management. The funds generated by this penalty charge would be returned to local government for the construction of solid-waste disposal facilities.

A national policy on resource management. And we must establish a national policy on resource management that puts a halt to the plunder of our mineral resources. This rape of the earth is being carried out in utter disregard for other values such as recreation, aesthetics, and the natural balance between man and his environment. Under any sensible resource plan, we never would have permitted undersea oil drilling until strict basic rules had been set up to govern the use of any marine resource. Now, the only sensible course is to halt all drilling in the Santa Barbara Channel—we know the area is too sensitive for exploitation—and to declare a moratorium on any new drilling anywhere on the outer continental shelf until we need the oil and have developed the technology to avoid a Santa Barbara type of disaster.

A national oceans policy. To avoid the greatest disaster of all—the destruction of all marine life—we must establish a national oceans policy to halt the use of the sea by cities and industries as a dumping ground for their wastes. In one year from the metropolitan New York City area alone more than 6.6 million tons of dredge spoils, 4 million tons of sewage sludge, 2.6 million tons of dilute industrial waste acids, and half a million tons of cellar dirt were dumped offshore.

A national policy of technology assessment. A new national policy also must be established that says the pesticides, herbicides, detergents, fuel additives—the plethora of products produced for a consumer society—will not be allowed in the marketplace until they are tested and meet environmental and health standards. In addition, we must take immediate steps to eliminate the slow-degrading "chlorinated hydrocarbon" pesticides. We must find an environmentally safe substitute for the polyphosphate base in detergents that is polluting our lakes and rivers. And (perhaps most important of all) if the air pollution from the automobile internal-combustion engine cannot be eliminated, the power of government must be used to force the transition to another engine, even if the substitute would mean a lower-performance automobile for a time.

A national policy on population. A national policy on population must establish and protect the right of every citizen to plan his family and to be fully informed of all the means of effectively and safely doing so. No plans to rebuild our cities, remodel our transportation system, update our waste treatment, or protect our open space will endure in the face of the rapidly expanding population that has been characteristic of the United States and nearly all other nations. If we cannot manage the wastes produced by 200 million people in this country, it will probably be catastrophic when we reach 300 million, as predicted, within the next thirty years.

A national policy of citizens' environmental rights. Finally, a national policy must be established that recognizes and protects every person's right to a decent environment. The individual now frequently finds himself with no remedy in the face of the pollution of a lake that belongs to the public, or the poisoning of the air that he must breathe, or the shattering din that is imposed upon him without his choice. To strengthen every individual's hand, I introduced early in 1970 a constitutional amendment which says: "Every person has the inalienable right to a decent environment. The United States and every state shall guarantee this right." If Congress passes this amendment, it must be ratified by three-fourths of the state legislatures before it becomes a part of the Constitution. With strong citizen support across the country, I am confident ratification can be achieved.

Restoring our environment will require on the part of the people this new assertion of environmental rights and the evolution of an ecological ethic of understanding and respect for the bonds that unite man with the planet's natural systems.

Make no mistake, ecology is a big science, a big concept. It is concerned with the total ecosystem, not just with how we dispose of our tin cans, bottles, and sewage.

Our goal is not merely an environment of clean air and water and scenic beauty. The objective is an environment of decency, quality, and mutual respect for all other human beings and all other living creatures. Our goal is a new American ethic that sets new standards for progress, emphasizing human dignity and well-being rather than an endless parade of technology that produces more gadgets, more waste, more pollution.

Are we able to meet the challenge? Yes. We have the technology and the resources. Are we willing? That is the unanswered question.

In my view, the natural stepping-off point for a national commitment for a new environmental citizenship was Earth Day. The massive involvement this nationwide event generated must be far more than a one-day affair.

As the next step we will need well-organized nonpartisan political-action organizations across the nation, building up from the local and state levels to launch a sustained effort to restore the quality of our environment. The sole dedication of these groups would be to campaign at every level of our society, taking positions, aiding candidates for office who support environmental programs, using every device within the political process to express the public's concern and to achieve environmental action. In our system sustained political action is the best method to implement the public will.

Up to now the decisions that have destroyed our environment have been made in the boardrooms of giant corporations, in the thousands of government agency offices protected from public scrutiny by layer upon layer of bureaucracy, and even in the frequently closed committee rooms of Congress, all by the consent of a lethargic public.

Now the matter must be brought out before the public and fought out in the political arena. To those who will say it cannot be done because "profit" and "progress" as we know them may have to suffer, I say that the cost of not acting will be far greater than anything we have yet imagined.

The Creative Approach to a Quality Environment

Lawrence Halprin

*When I went to Yale to give a talk on "quality in the
environment," I found it almost impossible
to focus on my topic.*

*It was the week following the tragic events
at Kent State University.*

*It was shortly after the United States had
invaded Cambodia.*

*It was six years after the beginning of
the terrible war in Vietnam.*

*It was in the echo of the polarizing speeches of
Spiro T. Agnew and a time of increasing inability to
communicate with the President or to feel that
anyone "up there" even cared.*

*Lawrence Halprin is a distinguished landscape architect and environmental
planner. His San Francisco-based firm has as its goal "the practice of environmental planning"; its achievements include the Comprehensive Design
Plan for the American Virgin Islands, the Sea Ranch on the California
coast, the Hebrew University campus in Jerusalem, Nicollet Mall in Minneapolis, and Ghirardelli Square in San Francisco. He is a recipient of the
Allied Professions Medal of the American Institute of Architects and a
member of the National Council on the Arts.*

It was in the time of a government that characterized
dissent as disloyalty and student activists as "bums"
and a climate of opinion where ghetto blacks
were being shot and Black Panthers were denied fair trial.

It was a week when the universities were all
being drained of the young people who felt these
universities had given up all pretense of
being relevant, and young people throughout the country
increasingly felt abandoned and unwanted—
even unneeded, except as cannon fodder.

It seemed to me a hard time to talk about
quality environment when so many more
basic issues lay before us.

And yet the environment is a basic issue.
It is a clear result of our own self-image—
an expression of where we are as a community.
It is what we are, and conversely, we are affected by it.
Environment is not a luxury.

The environment we live in influences us,
and our sense of community emerges from it.

There is a mutual feedback between ourselves
and how we live—one influences the other.

*The degradation of our environment is beginning
to affect and demean us all.*

*The terrible physical, financial, and emotional
limitations of the inner city demean all the blacks
in ghettos. They affect them in profound
psychological as well as physical ways.*

Pollution of our streams and air is poisoning us all.

*Increasing population is threatening the quality
of our lives.*

*The suburban sprawl and its partner, the automobile,
affect our life styles and the way we raise our children.*

*Our environment is beginning to close down
the options we have and is narrowing the potentials
of us all as human beings.*

*In spite of my difficulty in focusing, I nevertheless feel
that the environment* is *worth talking about—
it* is *relevant to us all.
It is* not *peripheral to our concerns.*

We do *need to preserve and improve it
so that it can improve us.*

*I believe we need to achieve an environmental quality
that is not derived from beautiful form but is based
on community content and community desire and action.*

*For me as an environmental designer
what really matters is how people become intricately
a part of environment—not only to enjoy being in,
but also to the extent that they are part of,
the activity of designing and building.*

*We all need to become ourselves, actively involved in
making places—our own communities as places
to live in and enjoy together.*

*We need to make the building of cities and regions
expressive of the sense of community
(not something done for private gain) and to allow
all the people to enter into community building as a
ritual act—an essential ingredient of the life act.*

*Environment then becomes, I believe, what it needs
once again to be—what primitive man understood it
to be—part of him and he part of it:
An aesthetic and ecologic symbiosis.*

(Technology will not solve our problems except as a tool.)

*It is we as humans, working together in community,
ritualistically, who can rechart the destructive
course of events and prevent the desecration of
our young people, our disadvantaged,
and the environment itself.*

*Many places I have designed are, I am told,
beautiful, but only some of those—for example,
the Portland Fountain—really feel good to me
because they make it possible for many kinds of people
to be included in the design in a creative and
involving way. They become part of the action.
The fountain does not exist outside of them. . . .
It is what they make of it. . . . It opens up options
and discloses possibilities.*

Lawrence Halprin

Lovejoy Fountain -- Portland, Oregon

In the plaza there should be events.... sculpture shows - concerts - dance events with dancers all over AND arriving to center space from above down stairs around fountain · - -

Sketch by Lawrence Halprin of Lovejoy Fountain, Portland, Oregon

This is a typed version of a letter Halprin received from Sherry Volz, giving her reaction to the Lovejoy Fountain along with comments she gathered from others at the fountain.

Dear Sir, (because I don't know your name)

I met your friend, Maude Dorr, at the fountain. Here are a few of the remarks I've gathered over the summer. I hope they bring you pleasure. Thank you for the fountain.

A wet Sherry Volz

(Guy age 17)–"It's real, like me, with so many personalities! I groove here."

(Young girl 13)–"I'm sort of scared of people, here I can do my thing, and if I have to talk to someone we can talk about the fountain."

(Boy 16?)–"Wow! It's just like Wow!"

(Woman 45 or so)–"I came to the fountain just to see it. I put my toe in and I was lost. I had to walk up the steps, dress, nylons, who cares? What a feeling! Such freedom."
(A woman from California on vacation)

(Little girl age 4)–(She steps into the lower pond, comes right out, runs fast while looking over her shoulder. She stops. She runs back into the pond. Repeats same over and over.)

I ask, "What are you doing?"

She points to her foot patterns on the cement and says, "The wet likes to follow me."

(Girl age 9)–(In Sunday dress) "It's okay if I get wet, it's okay. Mommy likes me to be wet."

(Boy age 8)–"I hate baths, when I come here she don't make me take one."

(Woman age 30)–"If I couldn't see, I'd come here just to listen and touch. It's a living creature, giving something of life to everyone."

(Father age 48?)–"I take the kids to the park, first I gotta push

them on the swing, then down the slide, up the junglegym—You
think I relax—Hell, no! The fountain, it plays with them. Me, I
relax—What more I want, heh?"

(Boy age 17)—"It's groovy, it sings, it screams, it whispers. I can
touch them all. Wow!"

(Girl age 8)—"Take me up the steps. Take me up the steps. Just
this once. Now take me down, oh please!"

(My thoughts age 24)—"The fountain is a special gift you give a
friend who has never been there. I like to give presents but I
don't have any money so I bring them to the fountain. It's nice
to give something you can't buy."

Thank you, sir.

/s/ Sherry Volz

(Photos courtesy of Maude Dorr, New York)

The Fountain

by Primus St. John

There is always some fountain
Where the water that really pouring—
Is our lives.
When I hear it,
I believe in all of the storms—
Where it came from.

Then, I make believe
I am one of those mossed backed prophets
That sticks on stone and waits
For everything—quietly.

"We are all pouring toward the same conviction,"
I hear the fountain say,
"But we believe that, separately."
So I believe it all—
The whole thing's that mindless,
And today is spring.

(*Pioneer Log,* Lewis and Clark College, April 3, 1970)

Can Technology Rescue the Cities?

Moshe Safdie

The industrialization of building is taking place whether we like it or not. It is as inevitable as the industrialization of agriculture. But what are the problems this industrialization of construction introduces to the environment? What are the issues confronting us within that process?

Industrialization will entail a complete reorganization of the building occupations. It will have implications on the way we manage land, plan our cities, and operate our legislative system.

The first obvious reorganization will occur at the level of corporate structure. Construction enterprises today consist of contractors, suppliers, raw-material manufacturers, architects, and engineers. With no really integrated structure, everybody is working on his own. Industrialization will not take place unless all these separate groups and disciplines are integrated into a closely linked organization. This would mean that, just as in the car, the aircraft, or any other industry, the people who design the final product also are involved in projecting the machinery and materials intended to fit particular requirements of that product. Research is undertaken and amortized over thousands of units of production.

As an example of the numbers I am talking about, consider an architect today. If he designs a house, he probably will charge 5 or 10 percent of its value for his efforts. By contrast, the funds spent in the designing of a single car model are about 10,000 percent of the value of one auto. Obviously, this is possible because the design costs are spread over hundreds of thousands of

Moshe Safdie, a native of Israel who was educated at McGill University in Canada, maintains architectural offices in Montreal. His design and execution of Habitat at Expo '67, the Montreal world's fair, was the first successful application of modular architecture in which interchangeable building units are predesigned and assembled on site. This and other plans for such projects as a moderate-income community of 800 housing units in Puerto Rico reflect aesthetic sensitivity while heralding a new age of industrialization and mass production.

cars. Still, we expect someone to put together a house that is really much more complicated than a car for only 5 percent while we devote 10,000 percent to a car!

Reorganization of the construction industry will mean that we must deal with a totally new realm of numbers. The quantity and level of decision involved in them would change. A fantasy exists that once we have building industrialization, all of our problems will be solved. Our current housing problems—our inability to afford enough new housing, or good enough housing, or a sufficient volume of housing—would be solved by the magic of technology. Such a mystique is very dangerous because it camouflages the threats that industrialization really introduces to the environment. Industrialization of the whole process of building is no guarantee of anything, and certainly not of good environment.

Imagine what might happen in the next ten or fifteen years if this industrialization took place. Try to picture the housing advertisements of 1984. A *Life* magazine ad published for the General Housing Corporation might read like this:

"Announcing the new super rancher for '84. Featuring dial view, exclusive with GHC. No windows. No daylight. Choose your own view in every room. Sealed interiors in our own filter-right air purifier. You can remove your gas masks when in the house. Wrist touch light; you need only touch your wrists and the lights will go on. New exclusive ooze-ite finish, gold or silver inside and out. The new infrablue kitchen. Special bonus for those buying this house in the first month: a one year's supply of GHC precooked Cavalcade of International Cuisine (three menus to choose from)."

Imagine a totally different circumstance—not GHC or some other supercorporation which has decided to go into housing because it is a good business. A 1984 ad in the *Washington Post* might go as follows:

"The Department of Housing announces that all heads of families born between 1950 and 1960, whose annual income is between $7,200 and $11,500, are now eligible for dwelling type G.H.K. in Zones 4, 5, and 11. Applicants should fill out form N. HUD-479Q84 in six copies. Also, those families living in Dwell-

ings B1 and C1 (distributed in 1980) may now apply for
washer-dryer equipment. Six copies of appropriate forms are
required."

Here are two completely different threats. But if we look at
the ads or the notices in some eastern European gazettes today,
we are likely to find amazing similarities to those above. And if
we take a present-day toaster or car advertisement and translate
it into housing, the 1984 *Life* ad does not seem exaggerated. It
points out this, too: if we assume that we will solve pollution
because it is unpleasant we are taking something for granted. It
might be cheaper in a distorted way to have everybody walk
around with little gas masks, and to seal houses and filter their
air. Or instead of going through all the effort of planning communities so that houses on exactly the right sites are exposed to
sunlight and have views, it might be easier to seal up the houses
and project the outside views to their interiors.

The options available to us are synthetic environments that
ignore everything we talk about in terms of conservation and
nature, or environments which we try to resolve from the real
problems introduced by technology.

The issues of building industrialization are three in number:
standards, density, and the design process—and how it is affected
by mass production.

Start with the issue of standards, or who decides what we are to
build for whom and how. Unlike ten, fifteen, or twenty years ago
when a builder bought up a few acres of land and subdivided
them and put up a half-dozen houses, the new age of mass-
produced construction means that someone would be making
decisions on the design of an environment that might affect
100,000 lives. If the traditional builder went wrong, his houses
just did not sell; either they were left vacant or he unloaded them
at a cheaper price. By contrast, a mistake in the new age of mass
production would affect thousands of people.

The second problem: small-scale construction implies a day-to-
day adjustment in the definition of standards. People earn a little
more, and they want a little better house. They go looking for it.
But who would decide the standards—a good house or a bad

house—if such decisions were made on a much larger scale than today?

I can find specific examples in my own experience, working with government, where this has become an issue that indicates what could happen in the future. Several years ago we were asked to apply the ideas of Habitat to public housing in Washington, D.C. We were called in to do some studies for it by the Department of Housing and Urban Development (HUD). We began with the premise that the government today spends $14,000 per house. We decided to figure out, within the constraints of this number, how good an environment we could produce. Our aims included an open garden for every dwelling, regardless of whether it was multistoried or would have community space in the street leading to the houses.

When we submitted our plans a very interesting debate erupted. Some of the HUD people said, "We did not ask you to change the standard of public housing. We were quite pleased with it. We feel it is quite adequate. We want to use technology to reduce costs, not to improve the quality of housing."

In reply, I urged that we try to improve the level of housing, because the experience and attitude of tenants to public housing in recent years prove that it certainly has not lived up to the expectations of anyone.

A young architect working for HUD countered: "Let's put it this way. We have 6 million or 10 million dwellings to build for low-income families in the next ten years. The difference between what you are talking about and what could be built is $5,000 a dwelling, is a total of $50 billion." His argument was that we could not afford $50 billion, which is one year's expenditure on the Vietnam War.

The question really boils down to this: What kind of an environment do we want? Who shall decide what it is going to be? How do we pay for it? What are the priorities for spending our money?

Another reminiscence from Washington really has more subtle overtones. A year later we were invited by HUD to work on the Fort Lincoln project, again in Washington, D.C. Three architects, each with a group of industries, were invited to make separate proposals based on the particular technology of their own industries. An aim of the program was to assess these and other proposals and decide what should be built on the site, which could accommodate 50,000 people.

Thomas Rogers was put in charge of this project. He was Director of Technology at HUD. A physicist, he was brought over from the Department of Defense in the hope that a scientist might bring some sense into housing and the environment. One day after we had started working he called us into his office and said, "Look, I am a physicist. I don't pretend to know very much about the environment. Here you are, three groups producing plans for buildings. How am I going to measure them? How am I going to decide which is best or which is worst? Obviously, it is not a simple matter of who is cheaper, because there are other variables to the environment. How shall I determine what we are getting for our money?"

The three architectural groups were headed by Paul Rudolph, Harry Weiss, and me. I think the attitude of Weiss—and I know of Rudolph, because he stated his opinion—was: well, really, you cannot measure architecture; if you do not know what it is all about go back to the Department of Defense. However, I felt that Rogers' question was reasonable. This is not to say that we could write a specification guaranteeing the results, but at least we could work toward meeting certain basic requirements.

After the meeting I tried to put down an environmental code (later I called it an environmental bill of rights) which includes about 150 items concerning goals that a community and a dwelling should achieve. I started with fundamental things. For instance, I said, a family should be able to reside in a dwelling and lead a normal life; that includes having parties, listening to loud music, and having quarrels from time to time without an audience of neighbors—or vice versa. This should hold true whether the tenants are living in a single-family house or a multistory structure. It is an uncompromisable requirement.

Among the points that followed was another of basic importance. It said that a young child should be able to leave the front door of his house and wander in an acceptable space and meet other children of his age without an adult standing watch.

Of course, if you take these points seriously, all the double-loaded corridor apartment buildings already built in this country become unacceptable. If you take my soundproofing requirement seriously, hardly any multistory form of construction could meet that standard today.

We are moving into a period in which many major decisions will be made at very high levels and will be almost irreversible. They will involve not only the consumer, who in the old days had some influence over purchases because he had some choice, but also high levels of government and industry. It has become absolutely essential to put down exactly what we want from the environment—the amenities, the needs, the requirements upon which we insist. That is a genuine political issue. We must expose it to deal with it.

I am working on a housing project in Israel that is also related to industrialization and the building of plants to manufacture houses. The same issue that arose in Washington came up in Israel. There were two factions in the Ministry of Housing. One group said, "We feel that the housing constructed in the last twenty years really constituted a rape of the land and has proved to be inadequate. We want to improve the level of existing housing. So this industrialized process should be aimed not only toward reduced costs and less expenditure of labor and material but toward making an effort to *increase* standards."

The other faction in the Ministry contended, "We are expecting very heavy immigration rates. We must house more people. If we cannot build enough housing, we cannot absorb immigrants essential to our national survival. We have great defense commitments. Our budgets are strangled. We should build minimum-standard housing. We should *reduce* standards."

This is a tough problem for Israel. The arguments cannot be labeled black and white. It is difficult to conclude that one faction is right and the other wrong. Indeed, perhaps both are right. Maybe we have to build housing that can be improved in later years because the buyers cannot afford high standards right now.

In the United States and in Canada the issue is quite different. In these countries it becomes a question of our ability to afford high "minimum standards" of housing and of our priorities. If we set down certain standards in black and white—not just in the jargon of planners and architects but so that physicists can understand them and they can be communicated to congressmen and the public—then we can insist that they must be met. If the economic system needs adjustment, these changes have to be made.

Another similar but really separate issue is the density question. The average density in which we live is one of the major factors causing change in the entire building industry and the whole environmental discipline. We underrate the impact of density on the processes of planning and of building. As we house more people closer together we change the environment or pose environmental problems in a quantitative way, as well as in a fundamental generic way. The housing of 100 people per acre is generically a different problem from housing one family on one acre.

Nor is this merely a question of quantity. We know that density has a tremendous impact on the environment; then, before going any farther, we should ask: "Why are we allowing ourselves to fall into a situation where we must build greater densities? Possibly we can avoid the whole difficulty by dispersing, by eliminating the form or the structure of cities that is forcing this density on us."

This is a complex subject, but I want to summarize my own personal conclusion of how I see the development of the metropolitan city today.

Every indicator of the metropolitan city suggests that it is growing in size. There are fewer and greater cities, rather than more and smaller cities. This process has continued for a long time and does not show signs of stopping. It has some basic social and economic foundations. Among them: people migrate to the big cities because they have wider choices in terms of their cultural and recreational life and of employment; industry and business move into cities to reach a greater source of specialists and to enhance their interdependence on each other. Without further

elaboration, I believe it is fair to assume that the metropolitan
city, in one form or another, is here to stay and that the metropolitan city, because of its size alone, underlines our inability to
continue low-density housing on this continent. This is plainly
impossible; statistically impossible.

I predict that we will undergo a fairly dramatic urban dispersal
in the coming ten or fifteen years. A revolution in our whole
mode of transportation will make this possible. In the next five to
ten years we will be introducing ground transportation systems
permitting travel at 300, 400, or 500 miles an hour. We will
eliminate air traffic for relatively short distances of 400 and 500
miles. These new methods of transit would mean that the size of
a city—formerly limited by the distance one could travel in an
hour—would expand. Today we can travel approximately fifty
miles by car in one hour; Los Angeles, Chicago, and New York
are about fifty miles in diameter. However, if we can travel 400
miles in an hour, we will be able to expand cities to a 400-mile
diameter.

Even though they will continue to disperse and (I hope) increase in numbers, these cities will nevertheless represent a dispersal of concentration. Not an even dispersal of a low-density
cheese spread over the environment but rather a concentration of
communities which are linked by high-speed transportation. At
any rate, let us momentarily take for granted the tendency
toward increased densities which is expressed in climbing land
values and in the fact that it is almost impossible to build any
more at low density in certain areas because land is simply una-
vailable.

The construction of a typical three-bedroom apartment in a
typical high-rise building costs no more than a house in a Levittown. But it does cost much more to build a high-density dwelling in a high-density context which has the same qualities of
environment as a low-density house.

Take a Levittown house as a standard measure of what we
consider to be middle-class America. If we were to ask the man in
the street today to define middle-income housing, or what he
regards as an average living environmental standard, a Levittown

house probably could be taken as an example. If we accept the suburban context of this Levittown house but examine it in terms of environment, I believe we could say that its occupants have a fair amount of privacy. It is separated by a brick wall and a six-foot air space from the next dwelling, which also has a brick wall. It has a garden that may be 600 square feet in size and can double as a play area. The street is a fairly safe and pleasant place for children to walk along, with a low traffic rate.

Take each of these facts and transfer it to a high-density context. For example, soundproofing. Translate the two walls with their six-foot air space to the context of a multistory structure in which two dwellings touch each other; at once we run into a costly, major technical problem to achieve the same soundproofing.

In the same way, consider the garden. Levittown land may have cost $1 per square foot. The Levittown garden is 600 square feet and costs $600. But provision for an open space of that size in a multistory structure, either on the roof or elsewhere will cost at least $5 per square foot or $3,000.

So what has happened to population density on this continent during the past twenty years? Those who could afford it stuck to the standard of the low-density environment. Those who could not afford it and were subsidized, and thus had no choice, were forced into a higher-density environment with a drastic decrease in environmental quality.

Now we face a new situation: the low-income family that was forced into a high-density environment is no longer prepared to accept it; the middle-income family cannot continue to spread at six families per acre. The implications of these facts are enormous. If we accept the premise that we are going to have greater density and agree that we do not want to reduce the quality of our environment, a much greater proportion of our income—either as a nation or as individuals—will have to be diverted to the environment. This means we must provide not just for housing but for the entire urban physical plant. There is no magic formula for achieving this, and there is no way to avoid the problem.

Industrialization of construction would make it possible for us to build more housing faster, and with less labor and maybe at reduced costs; but it will not close the gap between low and high density. A much greater expenditure of our income, of our Gross National Product, will be essential as the city becomes more densely populated, if we hope to retain an environment that we want.

Another implication of higher density is apparent when we examine our legislative and real estate traditions, both based on the traditions of a rural society. We still pretend that, if we own land, we can do with it as we wish. This is a huge fallacy, but at least we pretend it. The majority of this continent's population has a strong attachment for the concept of individual ownership of land. At the same time, in the urban context, we do not do as we may desire with our own land. We are dominated by zoning and building codes, as well as by many other rules, in the context of the total city.

Similarly, our planning tradition is a kind of two-dimensional rural tradition. We subdivide land, we build roads, and we separate the lots, and then build on those lots. However, in the context of a high-density city this is no longer workable. Think of any modern downtown area; consider the limitations imposed by the concept of subdividing land and putting up individual buildings. It immediately becomes obvious that in a context of the subdivision of land we cannot achieve a separation of the pedestrian from the car; a rearrangement of land uses three dimensionality so that housing and commercial areas are in their best positions, and interferences between functions are not created.

All of these make the implication quite clear: as density increases we have to accept the city as a subdivision of space, not as a subdivision of land. We must develop mechanisms or techniques to subdivide and plan and build three-dimensionally.

Truly, the implications are enormous because, in the urban context, they make obsolete the concept of private land ownership. Possession of a piece of space becomes more important than title to a piece of land. Within the concept of individual land ownership, the three-dimensional city is impossible. We have to start thinking of municipal rights-of-way in the air and not just on the ground. We must consider the possibility of creating great super-structures in which individuals and groups of people or corporations can build.

The third issue most directly related to the process of industrialization is what I call the tyranny of mass production. If one can generalize mass opinion, the public is fearful of what we call prefabricated housing. There is a connotation that prefabricated housing is really pretty awful. Architects tend to be irritated by that viewpoint, but in fact the public fear is quite justified. We have some examples, some advance warnings that this supposition is based on fact.

The country that has most industrialized its process of building is the U.S.S.R. It has been able to do this because its economy can be controlled on a large scale. It has what we call an aggregated market; in other words, it can assemble vast areas of land and build in great quantities. The Soviet Union has introduced more industrialization into construction than any other nation in the world. It has built at such a fast rate that it is closest to solving its housing problem.

On the other hand, a tour of Moscow's new suburbs, which were built through this industrialized process, is likely to leave the visitor with an impression that all was conceived by a single architect and his name is Kafka. The structures completely suppress the individual. There is no sense of identity. There is no scale of a person. Rather, identical buildings go on and on and on for miles in an endless repetition.

The same situation exists in the suburbs of Paris where the great French prefabricated systems have created mile after mile of painfully similar dwellings. This also is true in England and in the new towns of Israel.

We take too much for granted in North America if we assume that we will know better, because we may not at all.

Technology—where it has existed in building—has also created an environment that is not acceptable. A conflict is evident, because mass production in terms of the technology of today does mean standardization; it means repetition; it means everything that is implied by the stamping machine. A good environment, however, suggests that we have variety, that we have a choice as individuals, that we have a sense of location that does not confuse one place with another in the city. The rhythms, the variety in such an environment give us a feeling of well-being. It is very difficult to put a finger on the perception and use exact words to indicate what we mean, but we recognize a good environment when we are in one.

If we industrialize—and we will—we must understand the design issues that it introduces. We must accept our dependence upon mass production; we must acquiesce to repetition.

But how shall we develop methods that still will permit us to enjoy variety? How can we take similar elements and combine them into different permutations? How do we take houses and group them in varying ways so that each community has a distinct identity? How shall we design houses in which the individual has a choice, so that his house is not identical with the others; how can it be constructed so that its new owner may modify it to his particular needs and impose his own will on it? Dutch architect Aldo van Eyck calls this the architecture of numbers. If the problem existed before, it could have been only on a very small scale. Today it becomes necessary to invent a new vocabulary, to discover a totally new language of form and a whole method of using repetitive elements in a versatile way to overcome the threat of technology. This issue is not concerned merely with the level of building a house but also with that of a city, the largest scale of planning and control methods.

We could not comprehend any communication system today that did not rely on the highest level of control technology. In the field of communication this control technology has given us greater freedom than we have ever had. The direct-dialing telephone system is the best example. Technology—large-scale planning (and that is all it is: large-scale planning)—has made it possible for us to pick up a telephone receiver, dial several digits, and communicate with any one of hundreds of millions of individuals on this continent or overseas. Such planning in our environment, in establishing a new transportation system or in controlling our resources, could mean increased freedom such as we associate with the direct-dialing system. It also could mean, as it has in many countries, a suppression of individual freedom—like the public notice that announces our new home will be in Zone 2 and not in Zone 3.

One conclusion is apparent: the intuitive and often irrational process on which we have relied until now in designing the environment is not good enough. It is impossible for us to depend on the intuitive judgment of one individual or a group of individuals to tell us what a city or community should be like. Nor does it mean that somebody is going to be able to write an outline specification for a good community and put it in a computer and get the results. Our knowledge of what makes a good community, or a good city, or for that matter a good house is so limited that it will be a long time before any such purely logical and linearly rational process can be used.

In a sense, we must expand the meaning of "program." Thus, a program for a school is not merely a matter of specifications for 455 square feet for the chemistry lab and 300 square feet for the physics lab; we must start expanding the word to include all the aspects that make up a decent environment, whether they affect the quality of life or the flexibility of the use of space or the way in which people circulate. Whether it relates to physical aspects or psychic aspects of the use of the environment, we must expand that word program and try to increase the rational element in the design process.

Let me explain some of my efforts to achieve variety within the disciplines of certain production methods or mass production methods. I shall start with Habitat at Montreal's Expo '67. Although each example is in the context of a different economy, a different climate, and different technological capabilities, they all deal with a single problem: In what way can we respond to mass production in terms of individual needs?

The first Habitat proposal, when it was submitted to the Expo authorities, was designed for a community of 1,000 families. It was intended to replace the whole concept of individual national pavilions, to integrate land uses three-dimensionally, and to build a community out of single, repetitive, mass-produced elements.

The public facilities, the shops, the offices were sheltered by a membrane of housing composed of prefabricated space cells that had been completely produced in a factory and assembled in place. Here was the suggestion of the idea that each house should have a garden, that a pedestrian street should cross and link the community horizontally at various levels, and that the non-residential facilities should be related in one structure.

When it was built Habitat was reduced in size so that it could not really integrate all the public facilities, but still it tried to demonstrate that one repetitive space cell could be combined to make different houses of one, two, three, or four bedrooms and single or multiple stories—different arrangements grouped in a three-dimensional pattern and served by a system of pedestrian streets. On the public level were the plaza with shops, the meeting place, and so on. Each house had a garden and looked out in three directions so a resident would not feel cooped up as in a beehive, but rather as though he were floating in space. Pedestrian streets serving as links at every fourth floor were social spaces rather than corridors.

In the building of Habitat I was confronted with the question of whether a box element, put together in many different combinations, really meant variety. Isn't the geometry of the box so strong that it makes one house feel like the other? I have mixed feelings about that. There is really a great deal of variation in Habitat. But I decided to attempt to make houses that to a greater extent *feel* different spatially.

A system of six components (a cube with five subcomponents) could be combined to make all kinds of houses. Even though repetitive, the components included a round house and a cross-shaped house, a little "Arab" house, and a prism-shaped house. These, in turn, could still be grouped three-dimensionally to satisfy the requirements of structural loads and services; they could be a series of houses, each of which would feel different spatially and still would permit the owner to change to suit his preferences.

A project along New York's East River uptown called for a density of 300 people per acre. Could we satisfy what we felt about environment and what it should be in a context of 300 families per acre, ten times that of Habitat? The later design for the lower portion of the East River project went from the previous scheme to a suspension system, a series of mass-produced elements suspended off the major catenary fifty stories high and leaving the whole lower level open for offices, shopping centers, marinas, and other public facilities. We planned to have the modules produced in upstate New York, shipped down the Hudson River, and assembled to provide at least twenty different houses in the context of 300 units per acre.

The toughest problem we have faced was to achieve what we said was possible in the context of moderate- and low-income housing. Our first opportunity to do that was in Puerto Rico where we are working on a moderate-income housing project under the FHA 236 program. The proposal is for 800 units with all community facilities. A factory will be built to serve all of Puerto Rico, and the repetitive, mass-produced elements will be completely prefinished there. They will be shipped by truck or by barge and assembled at various sites.

The basic principle is that industrialized housing can be done only in the factory. The only way to produce construction in the factory is take the intended building and break it up into space cells that can be run off on an assembly line. The product must be small enough to transport but big enough to make sense as part of the house.

To make maximum use of the hill on which the Puerto Rican project is sited we are building clusters of twelve units with spiraling roads, parking under each cluster, and access upward or downward from the roads; thus, we can have high density without the use of elevators. Pedestrian streets also penetrate, linking cluster to cluster and making it possible to walk completely apart from vehicular traffic.

A three-bedroom house is being built for $14,000. With an FHA 1 percent mortgage program the tenants would be paying about $105 per month, including maintenance charges.

In a totally different context, we are constructing a resort in the Virgin Islands. It will be made in the same factory in Puerto

Rico, and will be shipped over for assembly on its site. Here the problem embraces a very beautiful peninsula in which the building method tries to preserve the terrain and the vegetation. The elements made in the factory will be quite different in shape and form from those for the Puerto Rico project. They must respond to a totally different program, and are arranged so that cylindrical units form columns and float the rest of the building. The result: minimum interference with the natural vegetation!

Israel poses somewhat different problems from the tropics climatically. People there spend a great deal of their life in their outdoor space, on their terraces. But seasonal changes bring rainy and cool winters and then very hot summers. So the inhabitants want the terraces to be shaded one day, open to the sky another, and enclosed with glass during the winter. Our attempt was to make a completely convertible outdoor space enclosed by a sliding dome-shaped window. The acrylic dome has a shutter for shade or a window to enclose the terrace and provide a greenhouse effect. The space can be converted from a shaded terrace to a glazed terrace to an open terrace at any given time.

For the first time we have combined concrete and fiberglass elements. The half-dome elements are space extended from the concrete elements. The structure itself is concrete, and the fiberglass element does not have to support anything except itself and need not be fireproofed.

A typical cluster here too provides for the separation of pedestrians and traffic and makes maximum use of the natural topographical qualities.

Two years ago I designed a student union for San Francisco State College. It posed a totally different problem from housing, because a union contains a dining room, a bookstore, meeting rooms, and a theater. This is not a simple matter of taking spaces within the context of a repetitive industrialized system.

Here, in capsule form, are some of the concepts. A building with 5,000 people entering simultaneously at lunchtime should not have a door as such; people should be able to walk up to the walls and through any window into any room.

A single bend can make a room the size of an office, a room

larger than that, a meeting room, a dining room, or the 10,000-square-foot theater. In each case, as the room gets bigger it gets higher.

Systems can extend beyond the process of building, and here we have a possibility for a vernacular kind of element so that students could make their own building to suit their own programs. They could make the rooms they need in the relationships they might require, but the special character of the building would be inherently the same.

A regulation by the trustees was that the building had to be compatible with the campus, which had been primarily designed by the California State Architectural Office in Sacramento. Although a little disturbed about this requirement, I did feel that the building had to relate to the rest of the campus and especially to the park in front of it. We planned to have the building completely covered with planting and become an extension of the park. This building, incidentally, is not under construction. The trustees have to approve the design, and for the past two years they have refused to do so.

One thought in conclusion. No planning idea or architectural environmental idea has meaning unless it can be translated into reality, which means political action. That is the key issue. We have all kinds of ideas, but do we have the machinery for implementing them? If we can translate certain physical ideas into legislation, we can bring about their realization and achieve environmental improvements.

This necessity for translation into political action exists at many levels. For example, if we conclude that people should spend more on their dwellings, then we could encourage anybody to spend up to a quarter of his income on housing and count it as legally tax-deductible expense. Or if we feel that we should have dispersal and new cities, we would create new urban regions where, for the first twenty years, no one would have to pay an income tax. People would go there because of that incentive.

For each physical idea there must be a counter political translation of it to bring it about. This is true at the levels of broad planning; it is also true of the scale of construction, except that in construction the obstacles to changing the process of building are enormous. There is a whole tradition of doing things in buildings that opposes industrialization, and it expresses itself in the pressure of unions and in all the many obstacles of existing systems. At the same time, taking it for granted that changes in the construction process will occur, we have no guarantee that we will get the environment we want from uncontrolled larger-scale industrialized building.

The concept of prototype, therefore, becomes very important. Only through the building of prototypes do we learn in other industries. A supersonic passenger aircraft does not go right onto the assembly line; first, one is put together by hand. And millions of dollars are expended on development plans before one is made by hand. Then it is flown for awhile, and finally—if it passes a multitude of tests—it reaches the assembly line. That is the process for supersonic transports; it is much simpler than the program for a community.

It seems to me that we must build complete communities as prototypes. This will require public funds and public support to bring it about, because it cannot happen on its own. It is going to take great resources to differentiate this, for example, from HUD's Breakthrough program which is intended to introduce new technology and change the building industry but ends up with systems that are being phased out after twenty years of use in Europe. (We are introducing them here as research programs.)

If we are going to have prototypes, funds must be provided for them; and I mean funds similar in magnitude to what we spend on space research and the Vietnam War. There is no other way. Unless we are prepared to appropriate such resources, I do not think we can bring about any real change in the environment.

Limits: The Environmental Imperative of the 1970s

Stewart L. Udall

It is noteworthy that in the seven months that have intervened since my opening statement this country has experienced a remarkable expansion of its environmental awareness. A president has devoted a major portion of a State of the Union address to the subject; the communications media have given it unprecedented attention; and the word ecology has entered the ordinary stream of conversation. These are significant gains. A successful campaign of education must serve as the seedbed of any idea that aims to transform our national life.

To be sure, there are many grounds for pessimism about our future these days. The doomsday prophecies of some ecologists and biologists make us uneasy. We are dismayed by the "benign neglect" philosophy of government, which asserts that inaction is the way to resolve our most urgent social and human problems. Unrest and skepticism trouble many students, and the seemingly unending involvement in Vietnam divides the nation and saps our moral resolve.

In a kind of Roman carnival atmosphere, we save our highest praise for robot machines and for men that circle the moon. President Nixon ecstatically opined that, "Nothing ever changed the world more" than the Apollo 13 mission to the moon. Months later we find that it did not change the world at all or contribute to a resolution of its crises. I am more convinced than ever before that the preservation of the human environment of this planet is far more important that further excursions to outer space.

The activities of the Environment Teach-In are now history. Critics are already busy with postmortem inquiries: Was it, some ask, nothing more than a tidal wave of rhetoric? Will it influence men and events? Was it, as *Newsweek* magazine put it, "a giant step or a spring skipalong?" It is too early to express judgment, but perhaps we would have been wiser not to have an Earth Day that would inevitably end up in a false climax and unnecessary drama. If we are to take farsighted action to begin to solve our environmental problems, we will require a long-haul commitment and the dedication of citizens in all walks of life.

During the nationwide observance of Earth Day some pluses were obvious, however. The discussion made us sharpen our awareness of many facets of the environmental crisis; it made us ask searching questions about the meaning of life and reexamine our concepts of the national purpose. On the plus side, too, many naturalist-type environmentalists were forced to recognize that any meaningful ecological program must begin in the worst slums of the cities and work outward to the wilderness, not vice versa.

The environmental movement has been strengthened by a convergence of many separate ideas or movements. We have witnessed in recent months a convergence of the family-planning movement with the environmental movement. The consumer crusade and the environment crusade have found themselves marching arm in arm. (After all, we consume not only products that we purchase at stores, but also the air we breathe, the water we drink, urban amenities—or disamenities—and all the myriad things that impact on our daily lives.) The conservation movement, of course, is the forerunner of the environmental movement—and if it has lost some of its back-country focus, so much the better for that.

Clearly the upwelling of the environmental movement has begun already to change the climate of public opinion. For example, look at the extraordinary degree to which opinion has crystallized and changed within the last year on the issue of abortions. I am convinced that the fresh arguments advanced by environmentalists for simple, humane abortion laws helped to produce a dramatic shift in sentiment. Among the notable recent actions: the New York Legislature has passed a model abortion statute, and the National Council of the Methodist Church has issued a ringing statement invoking ecological and moral reasons for very liberal abortion laws.

Perhaps the most important gain is that we are beginning to ask the right questions and to challenge basic assumptions that must be altered if we intend to make profound changes in the American way of life. To redirect technology, to redefine "progress," to win acceptance of a life style of restraint will not be easy. But we have started the right train of thought. That is what is important.

I still have a sinking feeling that inherent human weaknesses and the slow reflexes of government will carry us to the edge of catastrophes before we act with sufficient rigor. It may take large and small ecocatastrophes to galvanize action. But if we must have disasters and deaths to produce reforms, this generation will deserve indictment for its greed and lack of foresight.

In any event, I take some comfort in the circumstance that for the first time in our history the life sciences are up front. It was symbolic, I thought, when Dr. Vannevar Bush, one of the grand old men of an earlier era in science, said at the age of eighty that, if he were starting over, he would stake out a career as a microbiologist.

Clearly the environmental issues we are raising challenge the basic assumptions of politicians and leaders in business and industry. We have convinced many Americans that the production and consumption of goods are not synonymous with the good life. We have pointed out that it will take more than materialistic growth to sustain a life-giving environment.

The irony of our time is that each increment of the Gross National Product has gone hand in hand with a decrease in the livability of our cities and the cleanliness of the overall environment. It is little wonder that we are beginning to call into question the assumption that present patterns of economic expansion can continue indefinitely into the future or to doubt that further population increase will have beneficial effects on our society.

The growth projections almost fatalistically accepted by most Americans today are the source of the deepest misgivings of environmentalists. These self-fulfilling prophecies of the statisticians have a strong grip on the American mind. They convince us that there is little we can do to alter the course of history. Indeed, they picture our whole future with a deterministic framework.

Let us examine some of these projections. We are supposed to have 170 million automobiles by 1985 if present trends continue. (The automobile population grew four times as fast as the people population in 1969.) Yet no expert has stepped forward to tell us how our cities can absorb this auto increase, what it means in terms of a sharp rise in energy demand, or what effects it will have on human health. We are also told by the statisticians that our population will increase by 100 million people by the year 2000, that our need for energy will jump three or four times, and that our industrial system will require three times as many resources and raw materials. And we are asked to welcome with open arms another thirty years of suburban sprawl.

Frankly I am dismayed by this blueprint for tomorrow. It means we will lose the opportunity, perhaps for all time, to re-create a balanced, first-rate environment in this country. Looking at the world picture, it means that we will probably foreclose the aspirations of the developing nations for something approaching our materialistic standard of living. Can we continue into the foreseeable future to consume one-third of the world's energy, one-third of its resources—and produce one-third of its wastes and pollutants—without, in the end, imperiling the stability of the world community? I, for one, fear we cannot.

The environmental movement must raise profound issues about the present patterns of growth, about the future of life on this planet. It must also demand that we assert control before it is too late, and make those changes in our growth plans and in our individual life styles that will alter the path of progress.

The cutting edge of the environmental movement today is, therefore, a demand for change. People are opposing what we have called "growth" and "development" because that is the only way for them to express their concern at this stage. It is a holding action, yes; but in reality it is a demand for new goals and new directions.

I predict that it will spread and intensify. All over this country organized environmentalists are fighting superhighways that slice up cities, Corps of Engineers projects of all kinds, misplaced electric power plants and oil refineries, ill-sited chemical plants, and technological extravaganzas such as the SST.

As a case study, let us scrutinize the SST project for a moment. Up until now, what has been more American than the idea that, if a faster or bigger aircraft is to be built, American technicians will build it? Put simply, the supersonic transport demonstrates that modern technology is beginning to bump against the limits imposed by planetary laws, to encounter its own law of diminishing returns. On the one hand, the SST offers a modest travel-time gain for a small elite of "very important people." On the other hand, if it flies overland, it will blight the lives of 20 million or more citizens by a new form of environmental violence. It is an aeronautical Edsel; it can do nothing to shore up our "prestige" or our international balance of payments. It is an environmental Edsel also; and this is the reason ecologists have sought to make it a symbol of the fight to reorient technology now.

Yet, these head-on attacks on the industrial establishment were bound to produce a counterattack. It has already begun. Some business spokesmen are poking fun at "the ecology craze." Others are confidently predicting that the movement will run out of steam as soon as the public realizes the full cost of a quality environment. And some demographers are continuing to argue that the United States does not have a population problem.

We should welcome such debate. It will lead, hopefully, to a consensus and follow-up action on some issues—and to a continuing discussion of unresolved questions of high policy.

For my part, I am more worried about the blandishments of the quick-fix technology people than the negative arguments of the debunkers. Too many people are too ready to believe that science can readily adjust its sights and save us from the mess we are in. I have faith in science but little confidence in the potential of "science as usual" to rescue the environment. Certainly the track record of technology in the last decade does not inspire optimism: we perfected the space capsule but did practically nothing to advance the art of recycling wastes; we produced thousands of computers, but Detroit made no progress in manufacturing a halfway clean combustion engine.

We must face the fact that "reorienting technology" involves a national act of will geared to new priorities and Manhattan Project types of organizations. Anything less will result in empty promises and a fruitless spinning of wheels.

A few economists have also begun to snipe at ill-considered arguments being made by some environmentalists. We need a creative dialogue with the vital profession of the economists. We should make it clear that our quarrel with conventional economists and conventional economics arises out of a conviction that the time has come for changes in economic thought as profound and productive of change as those of John Maynard Keynes. The current economic system is based on ideology of maximum production and maximum consumption. It may have been appropriate in the past, but it could lead us down a path to disaster in the remaining years of this century. Can we continue to optimize indiscriminate growth and ignore those new concepts of growth that might create an optimum environment for man?

Is it right, we ask, for a nation that spends nearly 10 percent less in the public sector than some countries in Western Europe to assert that the *only* way our country can solve its social and environmental problems is by an unlimited upward spiral of the Gross National Product? If we fear that we are becoming a corpulent, acquisitive society, we must quarrel with the assumption that America can continue into the foreseeable future to consume so many resources while contributing so heavily to the pollution of this planet.

If the first law of life is change, the second must now be self-restraint and respect for the limits of life. The fragility and finiteness of the earth and its consumable resources must be a paramount preoccupation of the future.

The limits of power—and the necessity for mutual restraint— dominate the fateful United States-Soviet Union disarmament discussions at Vienna today. The idea of limits, I predict, will dominate not only the foreign policy of the world but its growth and development policies as well.

If the concept of limits becomes the environmental imperative of the 1970s, its programs and planning must include such elements as:

1. Plans and new priorities for the reshaping of cities and the extirpation of slums.

2. Drastic changes in individual life styles. The two-child family, the low-horsepower automobile, and a willingness to put limits on the consumption of goods, are only a few of the changes that will be required.

3. A nationwide plan to recycle and reuse all "wastes." We must have a resource recycling fund, based on national taxes imposed on manufactured goods and containers, combined with research that will produce a versatile technology of resource recycling. The earth's nonrenewable resources are limited, and these limits command the conservation and reuse of all irreplaceable resources.

4. Basic changes in our industrial-economic system that make "clean production" (as clean as technology can make it) and environmental protection an integral part of a new industrial ethic. This will require tough laws that are vigorously enforced and a willingness on the part of the consuming public to pay the extra cost of the superior products.

5. Development of a balanced transportation system. This will mean:

   High-speed ground transportation (probably tracked air-cushion vehicles) from city center to city center in all of the densely populated urban corridors of the country.

   Pleasant, convenient subways and mass-transit systems in all large cities.

   The conversion of some streets to people malls that will allow one-third or more of the urban residents to stroll or bicycle to and from work.

   The production by Detroit of a small, inexpensive, pollution-free "urban auto" designed for intercity use, not for cross-continent travel.

6. The development of a national land-use policy that will encompass open space, places for all kinds of inner-city play, and a national policy to promote the building of "new towns."

7. Billion-dollar research and development programs to solve urban and environmental ills featuring interdisciplinary

teams comparable to the efforts of NASA and the Manhattan project.

These are my random thoughts as one environmentalist who has
spent a very fascinating year on this campus and who believes
with Ohio physicist John R. Platt that the new generation is the
"hinge of history." Vast alterations of pace and attitude will be
required to achieve the enormous changes necessary to redirect
"the American way."

If we assume that present patterns of growth will continue, our
future is uncertain indeed. Can we change the system—and our
personal lives—fast enough? This is the overriding issue. It will
dominate our lives and torment the mind of the nation as we
search in the years ahead for a dynamic but balanced future that
respects the limits of life.